SPREADING THE GOSPEL AND THE SPIRIT OF PENTECOST

TO POSSESS THE NATIONS OF THE WORLD

VOLUME ONE

EWURAMMA

SPREADING THE GOSPEL AND THE SPIRIT OF PENTECOST TO POSSESS THE NATIONS OF THE WORLD

Copyright © 2023 by Ewuramma
All rights reserved.

ISBN: 978-0-9849805-6-7

Copyright © 2023 Our Paraclete. All rights reserved.

Published by: Our Paraclete, an imprint of Our Paraclete Publishers.

All rights reserved. No part of this book may be reproduced or transmitted in any form or by any means, electronic or mechanical, including photocopying, recording, or by any information storage and retrieval system, without permission in writing from the publisher.

Unless otherwise indicated, all Scriptures are taken from the Holy Bible, Amplified Bible, Classic Edition®, AMPC®. Copyright © 1962, 1964, 1965, 1987 by Biblica, Inc.™, used by permission of Zondervan. All rights reserved worldwide. www.zondervan.com. The "NIV" and "New International Version" are trademarks registered in the United States Patent and Trademark Office by Biblica, Inc.

Contact Author on:
ourparacletefoundation.inc@gmail.com

Design & Print by:
Indes Procom Ltd.
www.indesprocom.com

Cover Credit:
Richard Opoku Agyeman
Director, Acute Formula

CONTENTS OF VOL. I

Dedication — *v*
Apologia — *x*
Foreword — *xii*
Endorsements — *xiv*
Introduction — *xx*

CHAPTER 01
God The Father — *01*

CHAPTER 02
The Virgin Birth — *16*

CHAPTER 03
Jesus Christ's Procession — *45*

CHAPTER 04
Jesus Christ's Humiliation — *59*

CHAPTER 05
Contraction For The Birth Of The Holy Spirit — *68*

CHAPTER 06
The Conduct Of The Parturient Disciples In The Maternity Ward — *78*

CHAPTER 07
The Maternity Ward Of The Holy Spirit — *91*

CHAPTER 08
What Pentecost Is Not — *100*

CHAPTER 09
Not A Wholesale Salvation — *104*

CHAPTER 10
Evangelism Global Positioning Systems (GPS) — *116*

CHAPTER 11
Names — *137*

Epilogue — *156*
Acknowledgement — *159*
Welcome to our paraclete family — *163*
Appendix — *166*

Dedication

I dedicate this book to:

Apostle Professor Kwadwo Nimfour Opoku and Mrs. Grace Adwapa Onyinah
Fifth Chairman of The Church Of Pentecost 2008-2018

"O God, You have taught me from my youth, and hitherto have I declared Your wondrous works. Yes, even when I am old and gray-headed, O God, forsake me not, [but keep me alive] until I have declared Your mighty strength to [this] generation, and Your might and power to all that are to come." Psalm 71:17-18 AMPC

Professor Kwadwo Nimfour Opoku and Mrs. Grace Adwapa Onyinah do not require eulogy. "They have served the Lord God." is the best eulogy that could be given to them. However, the eulogy I offer them in the book is unquestionably well-earned. In retrospect, I give a lot of leeway to godly admiration, but gratitude has its own set of words. And it will be a mistake, if not a sin, to insert only a eulogy when a Christlike epitaph will be far more appropriate. So, I will include both.

So famous did then Apostle Opoku Onyinah become in the girls' dormitory of a secondary that each time school reopened, you would hear some little minds unconsciously give a very fragrant eulogy of the apostle:

"Aha, what is Apostle Opoku Onyinah saying anew?"

If Moses, Elijah, Paul, etc., were selected as mentors to people such as Joshua, Elisha, Timothy, Silvanus, Titus, etc., Mary, my childhood friend, would select Apostle Professor Opoku Onyinah as the man whose writings and sermons molded my life.

All the people I interacted with knew me as an admirer of Apostle Professor Opoku Onyinah. And there is power in the influence of admiration. There is no doubt that I looked (and of course, I still do) with loving reverence and admiration upon Apostle Professor Opoku Onyinah; for although young and ignorant about everything about God, I saw in him a virtue that won my heart's esteem and affection. Perhaps, even more notably, my friend, Mary, got the same inspired estimate of Apostle Professor Opoku Onyinah; hence, she calls him "Hannah's Apostle Opoku Onyinah".

No human tongue can possibly describe the ill experience of a priest of God who, after preaching the gospel to a congregation that appeared to be very receptive-hearted, discovered to their great chagrin that while they were away from the congregation, certain false teachers came in and turned them away from the gospel which had been delivered to them. That was Apostle Professor Opoku Onyinah's experience when, after God, through the leadership of the Church of Pentecost, had obliterated many idol worships, a small group of people in the church suddenly turned to Necromancy.

The church experienced a minor crisis as a result of those unbiblical practices. At the time when it felt necessary to sever many devout Christians from their association with the evil of Necromancy, Apostle Professor Opoku Onyinah, the main speaker at a Holy Ghost convention, on the theme "Life Abundant in the Holy

Spirit", so passionately condemned the practice of Necromancy and the like. He stated unequivocally that it is only as the Holy Spirit will keep both adults and children that we will be preserved from the infatuations of Necromancy and kept true to the grand old gospel of God. And even though I was still in Sunday school, Providence directed my steps to that convention.

From that Holy Ghost convention, Apostle Professor Opoku Onyinah won my admiration, and I started asking how I could get more of his sermons. I asked that people go to the headquarters of the Church of Pentecost in Ladadi, Ghana, West Africa, just to buy his sermons on cassette for me. And among his sermons was one entitled "Is this Naomi?" I listened to that sermon over and over until his words in the sermon became mine, and I started preaching it back to my mates. And after repeating the sermon over and over to them, they got the phrase:

"Aha, what is Apostle Opoku Onyinah saying anew?"

Although I am not a perfect human being, God made the Power of the Gospel appear in marvelous grandeur in my soul through Apostle Opoku Onyinah's sermons and books, particularly, *"Are Two Persons the Same?"*

I usually would go to the Challenge Bookshop to buy books of authors he referenced in his sermons, and the two that became my favorite were Watchman Nee and Tim LaHaye.

How powerful must the gospel be that once it has gained access into the heart of young children, it can never be taken out! Although I was a young girl who lacked knowledge, understanding, wisdom, and zeal at the time, the gospel began to make me grandiosely sincere in my arduous desire to serving Jesus Christ in whatever small measure I was capable of doing. The gospel of the Holy

Spirit that I heard from Apostle Professor Opoku Onyinah set my entire soul on fire. It gradually brought out God's gift that He graciously gave me over the years and developed everything that was concealed.

Persecution had followed persecution throughout the years, beginning with the false prophet who introduced "Necromancy", as well as his followers. But once I believed the gospel and resolved to holding on to it, it transformed me into a fearless soul. Like some Christians, I am willing to lose everything for the sake of the gospel. And as for all things, I regard them as excrement to win Jesus Christ.

The Holy Spirit continually unearths every gift that has been entombed in my life. He also propagates all the precious gifts of my mental wealth displaying them all to the honor of my beloved Jesus Christ who has purchased them all with His suffering, death, resurrection, and ascension.

To hold on to and spread the truth, I, like many other Christians, have faced rejection, loneliness, hardship, etc. However, none of those things moved me, nor do I regard my life as dear unto me, that I might be found in Jesus and to hear from Him on the last day say: *"Well done"*.

Papa and Mama Opoku Nimfo Onyinah, please, there are no words capable of conveying all that I feel. You are the very instrument God used to establish my friendship with the Holy Spirit. You are also the instrument by which God introduced me to the *Interpretation* of the Word of God. Mama Rebecca Baidoo was once interpreting a sermon you were preaching at a global conference held at the University of Ghana Legon, when I whispered: *"Oh, that God will enable me to interpret His Word."*. I am not sure what I would have done if the Holy Spirit, the Paraclete, had not become my Friend and given me His gift.

May the Lord God continue to bless you and strengthen your friendship with the Holy Spirit.

— Ewuramma

1. What can I offer to You, oh Lord
   For Your grace has taken me through
   I bring my sacrifice of praise
   For Your grace has done it again.
   Your grace has taken me through, oh Lord

   Refrain:

   Your grace has done it again
   Gracious One, I bow down to You
   Gracious One, I bow down to You

Apologia

At Pentecost, the Holy Spirit was the primary active agent in Jesus Christ's church's first manifest dedication and consecration. The Holy Spirit was the One who founded the church. He chose the early Christians, Pentecostalized them, and transformed them into living stones fit to be built together for God's dwellings by the Spirit. The Holy Spirit is the One who holds together those living stones because all Christian unity comes from Him as the Spirit of Peace, the Holy Dove sent forth from God after Jesus' accession. No Christian can ever forget those words:

"And when the day of Pentecost had fully come, they were all assembled together in one place, When suddenly, there came a sound from heaven like the rushing of a violent tempest blast, and it filled the whole house in which they were sitting. And there appeared to them tongues resembling fire, which were separated and distributed and which settled on each one of them. And they were all filled (diffused throughout their souls) with the Holy Spirit and began to speak in other (different, foreign) languages (tongues), as the Spirit [a]kept giving them clear and loud expression [in each tongue in appropriate words]" (Acts 2:1-4).

On that day, the risen Jesus, having obtained gifts for men, fulfilled the old prophecy by the prophet Joel:

"And afterward I will pour out My Spirit upon all flesh; and your sons and your daughters shall prophesy, your old men shall dream dreams, your young men shall see visions." (Joel 2:28).

Thus, the key distinction between a Christian and a non-Christian is that the Christian knows the Holy Spirit because He is with them and dwells in them, and they are, thus, Pentecostalized. Every Pentecostal Christian's ruling power delights in the gospel and the fellowship of the Holy Spirit. Their entire life becomes their religion, and their religion pervades their entire life. Pentecostalized Christians eat rice and chicken stew or fufu and palm nut soup as religiously as they partake in the Lord's Supper. They speak the truth in their Hair Salon as religiously as they do in the Church. Whatever a Pentecostalized Christian eats or drinks or does, it is all done to the glory of God. The main thought a Pentecostal Christian has when waking up from bed until going to bed, walking into their workplace, schools, hospitals, church, marrying, nursing their children, relating to friends and neighbors, and even taking recreation is:

"How can I glorify God, Jesus, and the Holy Spirit in all that I do?"

Everything about a Pentecostal Christian is given over to the Holy Spirit. Their body, spouse, children, home, money, and time all serve to glorify God.

FOREWORD

All throughout history, the Pentecostal movement has been recognised as the fastest spreading strand of the Christian faith. Pentecostalism has a lot to do with experiencing the power of the Holy Spirit as recorded in the Acts of the Apostles.

What has kept the Pentecostal fire ablaze in all generations has been an emphasis on, among others, trinitarian balance, the depravity of humanity, the person and ministry of Jesus Christ, the person and ministry of the Holy Spirit (including tongues-speaking and the operation of spiritual gifts), the need for repentance, holy living, aggressive evangelism, and a consciousness of the return of the Lord Jesus.

The transition of a sinner into a saint and into a steward of God's unfathomable mysteries is a massive enterprise undertaken successfully only by God himself and with the co-operation of the individual. The transformed soul now becomes a tool in God's hand to spread the gospel to others.

In "SPREADING THE GOSPEL AND THE SPIRIT OF PENTECOST TO POSSESS THE NATIONS OF THE WORLD", Ewurama beautifully shares her understanding of the dynamics within the Godhead and its implications for the salvation of humanity. Each of the twenty four chapters touches on very core biblical truths underpinning salvation and the new life in Christ. Her conviction is that real life in Christ Jesus is the life of the Spirit - the Spirit of Pentecost. The presence of the Holy Spirit freely given to the believer must manifest in a transformed life and a passion to serve the Lord Jesus Christ through the spread of the gospel. Hence "possessing the nations" is a natural consequence of a fired up Christian.

I have known Ewuramma for about thirty years. Her Pentecostal fervour has not dimmed all these years. She is multilingual, a consummate interpreter, and a skilled writer. To say that she is prayerful is a modest assessment of her spiritual discipline. Her passion for the study of the scriptures is par excellence. Indeed this book is a testimony of that devotion to the Word.

I recommend this book for anyone who seeks to understand their salvation and the assignment accompanying it. New converts (and even unbelievers) may also find this book a very useful material to aid their journey of faith. For church members and leaders, this book is a must-have.

May the Lord Jesus light fire in our hearts by the Holy Spirit as we seek to grow in grace and knowledge of the truth.

Apostle Dr. Ben Debrah
National Head, The Church of Pentecost-Sweden

Endorsements

The book ignites in us a profound hunger for the widespread and dissemination of the gospel as it clearly demonstrates the respective distinctive roles of God the Father, God the Son, and God the Holy Spirit in the conversion of souls.

The book vividly underscores the pressing need to saving human souls offering practical guidance as depicted by those involved in rescuing individuals affected by natural disasters. It establishes the proclamation of the gospel of Christ as a litmus test for every Christian emphasizing that a saved soul should never be ashamed of sharing this message. It also underscores the truth that the genuineness and significance of our salvation become evident through our approach to spreading the gospel of Jesus Christ.

This holistic Gospel propagation book has the potency for an impactful possession of nations for Christ Jesus.

Apostle Dr. Frank Asirifi
National Evangelism Director
Church of Pentecost USA

This book is an intense research work about the nature of the Godhead - Father, Son, and the Holy Spirit - in simple language that is easy for assimilation by everyone. Special detail is given about the suffering of Christ, His life, ministry and impact. Volumes of detail about the Holy Spirit and His help in transforming the raw gospel into a saved soul is covered. Various related concepts are explained with cogent illustrations to create a lasting impression.

The book is a great resource for the unbeliever, the new believer, the questioning believer as well as the seasoned believers.

Elder Philip Asare
District Secretary
Church of Pentecost New York.

This book emphatically tells about the deity of God in the person of Jesus; His birth, His life, His Death, His Resurrection, His Ascension and His Second Coming. It enlightens one to know the purpose for which he/she lives and to understand his/her mission on this planet.

The book also depicts the life of Christ our Savior, and the Holy Spirit our Helper who also reveals mysteries of the Gospel for us to be grounded in Him.

The Power of the Holy Spirit breeds the Pentecostalism in individual's life. Personally, the Holy Spirit prompts and enables me to be vigilant in everything I do in my Christian journey. Beside Him, no other god or human being can be relied upon.

Jesus's mission is for mankind to be saved from their sins due to humanity's depraved nature. Further, the clarity of the book tells how valuable the blood of Jesus is, such that it cleanses the sins of human beings.

The book also teaches how to evangelize the unredeemed. It is designed for all to differentiate light from darkness causing every believing soul to come to the saving knowledge of Christ. So, I entreat each and everyone to read this book to be much knowledgeable about God's supremacy.

Deaconess Lilian Martey
New York Region Witness Secretary
Church of Pentecost New York

I am humbled and pleased for the opportunity to give an endorsement of this great piece of Christian Literature.

Ewuramma is a staunch believer of Jesus Christ, a Preacher of the Gospel, a Life Coach, a Theological Researcher and a purpose-driven woman of great faith and prayer. She has authored many Christian Literature such as **Spring Up 'O' Well (Abura), As It Was In The Beginning,** among others.

In this book, ***Spreading the Gospel and the Spirit of Pentecost: To Possess the Nations of the World,*** the Author has provided a succinct account and explanations of how the Godhead worked and continually works in unison from the time of creation till these contemporary times of ours.

By grabbing a copy of this book to read, you would get to appreciate the roles of the Holy Spirit in the Godhead, His role in the Virgin Birth of Jesus Christ, the powerful and mighty manifestations of the Holy Spirit in the propagation of the Gospel and the life of Mankind, among others.

For me, the two most intriguing parts of this book you would yearn to read and know more about are the:

i.   Contraction for the Birth of the Holy Spirit and
ii. The Maternity Ward of the Holy Spirit

The book seeks to provide answers to many of your nagging questions on the subject of the Holy Spirit and who He is.

I can assure you this book will impact you, your generation and generations yet unborn.

Spreading the Gospel and the Spirit of Pentecost: To Possess the Nations of the World has been authored for everyone – the believer and unbeliever.

I highly endorse and humbly recommend this book to all children of the Kingdom of God – infants, teens, youths, adults, novices (like the Ephesian Believers) and veterans – seeking to know and experience the Power of the Holy Spirit.

Mrs. Henrietta Anim-Ansah (née Amoako-Asante)
U.S.A – Yonkers, NY.

Hello, my fellow brother/sister! Let me explain to you the miracles of Jesus Christ. Jesus was sent to this Earth by God. Keep in mind, God is One in Three forms: God the Father, God the Son, and God the Holy Spirit. God sent His Son Jesus to be a Guide in our lives. John 3:16 backs this up as evidence.

I watched this YouTube video saying Jesus is like a "Christmas praise". When you open a gift on Christmas Day, you say: "Thank you mom." or "Thank you dad." And when you open a huge gift, you say: "AAH— YES LORD!!" I'll tell you why Jesus deserves your Christmas praise. There's a dinner called "The Last Supper". One of the twelve disciples betrayed Jesus. It was Judas Ischariot. According to the gospel of Matthew, Judas immediately regretted his actions and returned the thirty pieces of silver to th church authorities, saying: "I have sinned by betraying innocent blood." (Matthew 27:3-8).

Jesus was beaten brutally. However, the worst of it all was they nailed Him to a wooden cross. Surprisingly, Jesus decided not to curse them. Instead, He said: "Father, forgive them, for they know not what they are doing." The real reason for this was because we all were sinners since we came out of the womb of a woman. Jesus shed His blood so that we wouldn't go to hell. This is why Jesus deserves your praise and worship. This is the least you can do. Please, don't fear if you make more than one mistake. The summary of these quotes: Isaiah 41:10, Psalms 37:4, and Jeremiah 29:11 says basically that we should not fear because Jesus is on our side and He wants us on His side.

Derek Owusu
Pre Youth, Bethel District Church of Pentecost

Salvation is the deliverance from sin and is to be brought by having faith and believing in christ the lord. The sacrifice of jesus is a both the salvation from God and the offering of the son, Just like the salvation of zacchaeus when jesus entered jericho and was passing through in the crowd.

Mary Elizabeth Gyamfi
Church of Pentecost New York District Sunday School

Introduction

Although He is the most active, powerful, and real worker in the universe, THE HOLY SPIRIT is not acknowledged by many Christians. Unfortunately, many contemporary Christians, like the Ephesian believers, have believed in Jesus Christ and have been baptized in the name of the Father, the Son, and the Holy Spirit, yet they seem to have not so much as heard whether there be any unmatched power of the Holy Ghost.

"And he asked them, Did you receive the Holy Spirit when you believed [on Jesus as the Christ]? And they said, No, we have not even heard that there is a Holy Spirit". (Acts 19:2).

The Godhead is made up of three persons: the Father, the Son, and the Holy Spirit; those three are one God, equal in substance and power and majesty. The name of God is plural in the narrative of creation: *"Let us make man"* — and the work of creation was the doing of the Godhead.

The doctrine of the Holy Trinity is most clearly portrayed in Genesis; when God created the world, the Holy Spirit hovered over the water, and God the Father spoke the Word (Son) to create. (Psalm 33:6; John 1:1-2).

God repeatedly reveals the Divine Persons as He declares He has set His Son on His holy hill of Zion:

"Yet have I anointed (installed and placed) My King [firmly] on My holy hill of Zion." (Psalm 2:6).

Or when He promised He would pour out His Spirit upon all flesh:

"And afterward I will pour out My Spirit upon all flesh; and your sons and your daughters shall prophesy, your old men shall dream dreams, your young men shall see visions." (Joel 2:28).

We find many traces of the doctrine of the Trinity in the context of the New Testament. And while every work of Divine Power is attributed to God, each of the blessed Persons of the Trinity has a particular office and agency in carrying it out. Thus, before Jesus Christ began the work of salvation, God the Great Preacher preached from heaven using the Holy Spirit (Dove) as a pulpit; one of the great sermons:

"And there came a voice out from within heaven, You are My Beloved Son; in You I am well pleased." (Mark 1:11).

So, God the FATHER is always regarded as the Guardian of the Godhead's rights and honors, and thus, as the Supervisor and Authorizer of the work. Thus, when the world, unfortunately, went astray due to Adam's fall, with the world convicted and condemned and the world given over to perish, there was the need for intervention because of the world's transgressions. Nonetheless, the fall of Adam and the ruin of humanity created abundant space and possibilities for divine love. There was space among the wreckage of humanity for God to demonstrate how much He loves humanity.

God, therefore, sent His only begotten Son into the world. He devised a way to show His infinite love to a sinful world through the plan of mercy, and the immense Gift (Jesus) required to carry it out. God demonstrated His love to the world through the Gift

- His Only-Begotten Son, in that while we were still sinners, Jesus Christ died for the ungodly in due time.

"But God shows and clearly proves His [own] love for us by the fact that while we were still sinners, Christ (the Messiah, the Anointed One) died for us." (Roman 5:8).

Jesus Christ is God the Father's only begotten Son, the beloved Son in whom the Father is well pleased. God the Father offered His Other Self, one with Himself, when He gave Jesus to the world. God's Gift in the person of the Son (Jesus) became incarnate, worked righteousness, and atoned for sin, declaring: "It is finished!" when the atonement was completed. After completing His part of the salvation work, Jesus Christ did not need to stay on earth any longer because His work below was forever accomplished. God the Father declared Himself delighted with His obedience in the role of a Servant and exalted Him to His own right hand, and given a name that supersedes all.

"And after He had appeared in human form, He abased and humbled Himself [still further]and carried His obedience to the extreme of death, even the death of the cross! Therefore [because He stooped so low] God has highly exalted Him and has freely bestowed on Him the name that is above every name..." (Philippians 2:8-9).

After Jesus Christ's work, there remained still a choice favor reserved to grace humanity in the salvation plan, with the highest honor to His triumphal ascension:

"Therefore it is said, When He ascended on high, He led captivity captive [He led a train of vanquished foes] and He bestowed gifts on men." (Ephesians 4:8).

God could not have bestowed the gifts of the Holy Spirit to humanity until Jesus' triumphal ascension into heaven.

"Being therefore lifted high by and to the right hand of God, and having received from the Father the promised [blessing which is the] Holy Spirit, He has made this outpouring which you yourselves both see and hear." (Acts 2:23).

Thus, God has given humanity two magnificent Gifts: the First is His Son, and the Second is His Spirit. After the First Gift (Jesus) was fulfilled, it became necessary for Him, whose person and work comprised that precious blessing, to remove Himself so that He may have the ability to spread the Second Blessing, through which alone the First Gift becomes of any use to humanity.

JESUS CHRIST (Son) reveals God's plan for salvation. Through His (Jesus) personal sufferings and obedience, He supplies the atonement and righteousness that justifies the Father in forgiving the sinner and restores them to sonship. Thus, He (Jesus) works as an intermediary between mankind and the God whom we had offended but to whom we would reconcile.

The HOLY SPIRIT prepared human nature for the incarnation of the Son (Jesus). He helped Jesus Christ in carrying out His mission on earth through obedience and suffering.

The Holy Spirit then equips, convinces, and motivates the sinner to accept salvation and follow Jesus Christ. The Holy Spirit enlightens the sinner's intellect to understand the truth revealed by Jesus Christ. He transforms their corrupted heart to love the truth and strengthens them in all His might to obey and walk in truth. Thus, salvation is the work of the Father, the Son, and the Holy Spirit, and we should give equal appreciation to the three Persons of the Godhead. However, just as the Father's purposes would be incomplete without the Son's work, the Son's work would be unsuccessful without the application of the Spirit.

Without the work of the Holy Spirit, the crucified Christ will be of no functional use to humanity; and the atonement that Jesus did can never save a single person unless the Blessed Spirit of God applies it to the heart and conscience.

As in the first creation, God created the world through His Son (Jesus), as the WORD of His power, but it was the Holy Spirit who moved upon the face of the waters to bring order out of chaos and light out of darkness; similarly, in the new creation of humanity to holiness, the Word of God in His Son's Gospel does not prevail until the same Spirit has moved on the corrupt and dead soul arousing it to a new and righteous life.

We are in the dispensation of the Second Gift, the advent of the Holy Spirit. All the impacts of the Gospel on our hearts are, thus, to be attributed to the Holy Spirit's power:

"For it is through Him that we both [whether far off or near] now have an introduction (access) by one [Holy] Spirit to the Father [so that we are able to approach Him]." (Ephesians 2:18).

Thus, the Gospel of Jesus Christ is indeed the Gospel of the Holy Spirit.

CHAPTER 01

GOD THE FATHER

The doctrine of the Trinity in Unity is not found in the Bible in formal language. Yet, it is kept in solution throughout the Bible in so many ways and words. Trinity is mentioned unintentionally, combined with other facts in the Bible that make it extremely remarkable as if presented in a specific definition. The writers of the New Testament have brought Trinity to the attention of Christians in so many instances that we may be willfully oblivious of if we do not notice it.

Apostle Paul specifically names each of the three divine Persons and each Holy Person as being involved in the operation of salvation:

"And because [really] are [His] sons, God has sent the {Holy} Spirit of His Son into our hearts, crying, Abba (Father)! Father!" (Galatians 4:6).

In plain terms, the Father (God) sent forth His Son (Jesus Christ); the Son redeemed (redeems) those who were (are) under the law; and the Holy Spirit entered (enters) the hearts of believers causing them to cry Abba, Father. In coming to save humanity, Jesus Christ made it a part of His mission to reveal the Father to us. Humanity must know God to be saved, and therefore, Jesus Christ of Old promised that:

"All the ends of the earth shall remember and turn to the Lord, and all the families of the nations shall bow down and worship before You…" (Psalm 22:27).

The phrase "name" is a remarkably powerful word in the Bible encompassing all that properly represents a person or a family. In the case of God, it comprises the entirety of His Deity, and Jesus Christ came to fully reveal Him to us. Thus, Jesus revealed to us the Divinity, the nature of God, the character of God, God's work, and God's revelations.

Jesus Christ referred to God as *"…righteous Father", "Father",* and *"Holy Father"* on different occasions. God is "righteous" with the attributes of a Judge and a Ruler: just, unbiased, and without mercy to the guilty. Yet, He is "Father" – close Relative, Caring, Compassionate, and Forgiving. He combines the two attributes in His personality and relationships with His children.

After announcing His impending departure, Jesus consoled His disciples with the words:

"Do not let your hearts be troubled (distressed, agitated). You believe in and adhere to and trust in and rely on God; believe in and adhere to and trust in and rely also on Me. In My Father's house there are many dwelling places (homes)…" (John 14:1-2).

Then Jesus replied:

"…Have I been with all of you for so long a time, and do you not recognize and know Me yet…?" (John 14:9).

Thus, Jesus purports to be the Father's Revealer. As the Everlasting *"Logos"* or *"Word",* He serves as a bridge of communication and friendship between God and man just as language serves as a means of conversation between one human being and the other. In every way conceivable, Jesus' incarnation, when the Word became flesh, was the Utterance of Divine Conversation with humanity in that the Father revealed Himself to us:

"All things have been given over into My power by My Father; and no one knows Who the Son is except the Father, or Who the Father is except the Son and anyone to whom the Son may choose to reveal and make Him known." (Luke 10:22).

Our unassisted thoughts of God the Father before the coming of Jesus Christ are blurry and inadequate until Jesus clearly revealed the Father. He showed us the glory of God because it shone in His own face.

"And the Word (Christ) became flesh (human, incarnate) and tabernacle (fixed His tent of flesh, lived awhile) among us…" (John 1:14).

When Jesus told His disciples that He was about to return to the Father's house and that they knew the way, Thomas said:

"…Lord, we do not know where You are going, so how can we know the way?" (John 14:5).

To Thomas, Jesus replied:

"I am the Way and the Truth and the Life; no one comes to the Father except by (through) Me." (John 14:6).

In other words, He came to reveal God and provide a pathway for the lost to return to their Father. Through the atonement on the Cross, Jesus constructed the way. At His crucifixion, Jesus spread out His pierced hands towards the Father on one side and the sinner on the other; thus, the atonement was accomplished. So, the sinner is restored to the Father's house:

"…I will come back again and will take you to Myself, that were I am you may be also." (John 14:3).

Similarly, we may readily understand Jesus Christ's deep teaching of prayer.

"Up to this time you have not asked a [single] thing in My Name [as presenting all that I Am]; but now ask and keep on asking and you will receive, so that your joy (gladness, delight) may be full and complete. I have told you these things in parables (veiled language, allegories, dark sayings); the hour is now coming when I shall no longer speak to you in figures of speech, but I shall tell you about the Father in plain words and openly (without reserve). At that time you will ask (pray) in My Name; and I am not saying that I will ask the Father on your behalf [for it will be unnecessary]." (John 16 24-26).

And yet, in one other greatest scenario, Jesus prayed to the Father for them. He prayed for the Comforter's continued presence.

"And I will ask the Father, and He will give you another Comforter (Counselor, Helper, Intercessor, Advocate, Strengthener, and Standby), that He may remain with you forever-" (John 14:16).

Jesus also taught His disciples to pray to God, perceiving Him not only as a Father through creation but also as a Father through adoption and the new birth:

"...Our Father Who is in heaven, hallowed (kept holy) be Your name." (Matthew 6:9).

Thus, Jesus taught the disciples that they were more than God's creatures: they were adopted into God's precious family. He adopted them from the old corrupt family in which they were born. God cleansed and purified them, gave them a new identity and Spirit, and made them new.

"And if we are [His] children, then we are [His] heirs also: heirs of God fellow heirs with Christ [sharing His inheritance with Him]; only we must share His suffering if we are to share His glory." (Roman 8:17).

And all of the processes of salvation are due to His free, sovereign, gratuitous, and distinguishing grace. And, having adopted them as His children, God has regenerated them through the power of the Holy Spirit.

The Father-child relationship also involves love. If God is my Father, He loves me. And oh, how He loves me! God is the best of fathers.

GOD THE SON

God the Father spoke only three brief words about His Son during the transfiguration, each of which could be regarded as very profound:

"...and a voice from the cloud said, This is My Son, My Beloved, with Whom I am [and have always been] delighted. Listen to Him." (Matthew 17:5).

"This" was used as though God were diverting Peter's, James', and John's attention away from Moses and Elias by saying: "*This is He of whom I speak to you.*" He is my Son, and He is greater than the law and the prophets."

The relationship between Father and Jesus Christ is explained in minute detail in His proclamation. The Father's words are ones of manifestation and peculiarity, in which He distinguishes the Son from all others as His closest and dearest Son.

As creatures of God, created in His likeness and after His image, humanity, as a whole, has a sense of relationship with God. But there is another sense in which Christians are adopted into the household of Christianity after accepting Jesus Christ, such that we might say: *"Abba, Father" (Galatians 4:6).*

Because Jesus Christ is not a Son by creation or adoption, but by birth, He and He alone is referred to be the Son of God: *"the only begotten". (John 3:16).*

Above all others, and in a unique way, Jesus is greater than all the angels:

"…For to which of the angels did [God] ever say, You are My Son, today I have begotten You [established You in an official Sonship relation, with kingly dignity]? And again, I will be to Him a Father, and He will be to Me a Son?" (Hebrews 1:5).

We do not understand, and cannot fathom, the doctrine of the Son of God's eternal parentage. And it may be almost sinful to try to peek into that glorious mystery: a sacred subtlety prohibits it, and the radiance is too bright: we lack the eyes that could discern anything in such a flash of light. However, we can see that Jesus is not simply the Son of God in the sense that the concept corresponds properly with sonship among mankind because He is coequal and coeternal with the Father: and Jesus is:

"…and His name shall be called Wonderful Counselor, the Mighty God, the everlasting Father [of Eternity], Prince of Peace." (Isaiah 9:6).

He is not lesser than the Father, for Jesus was with the Father at the beginning of creation and was very active in the work of creation:

"In the beginning [before all time] was the Word (Christ), and Word was with Gods, and the Word was God Himself" (John 1:1).

Thus, God at the transfiguration personally designated Jesus the Son as being present, separated Him from all others, and set Him apart as the sole and only one, and no one else may claim the appellation: *"This is my beloved Son."* He emphasized Jesus Christ's presence there and then, not as a future event, but as a present presence with the disciples, their Shepherd, Savior, and Friend: *"This is my beloved Son."* The Father's hand was not pointing into history, but His hand was on the actual Savior who appeared before them in flesh and blood, and of whom they later remarked:

"For it is written, You shall be holy, for I am holy. And if you call upon Him as [your] Father Who judges each one impartially according to what he does, [then] you should conduct yourselves with true reverence throughout the time of your temporary residence [on the earth, whether long or short]. You must know (recognize) that you were redeemed (ransomed) from the useless (fruitless) way of living inherited by tradition from [your] forefathers, not with corruptible things [such as] silver and gold…" 1 Peter 1:16-18)

While Elijah and Moses appeared on that Mountain, Jesus Christ stood among His apostles, and the Father pointed Him out, saying: *"This is my beloved Son."* They could make no mistake whatever about the person: the words of the Father so distinctly pointed His Son out.

Based upon the teaching of God the Son, there is another profound promise given to His disciples which refers to their own service and equipment

"Verily, verily, I say unto you, he that believeth on me, the works that I do shall he do also; and greater works than these shall he do; because I go unto my Father." (John 14:12).

That is explained by the fact that Jesus went to the Father in order to send them the Holy Spirit to prepare them for service. It is obvious that the greater works to which He referred were not miracles of healing since as a matter of fact, their miracles of healing were not greater than His. The reference is to the pre-eminent miracle of bringing souls to God. The visible results of the evangelism of Jesus during His ministry were comparatively meager.

Jesus' promise was:

"Ye shall receive power, after that the Holy Ghost is come upon you:" (Acts 1:8a KJV).

And that was a perpetual gift as Jesus said:

"And I will pray the Father, and He give you another comforter, that He may abide with you forever." (John 14:16).

God The Holy Ghost

The disciples of Jesus Christ faced a difficult assignment. They were to go throughout the world and preach the gospel to all creatures beginning in Jerusalem, Judea, Samaria, and to the ends of the world:

"But you shall receive power (ability, efficiency, and might) when the Holy Spirit has come upon you, and you shall be My witnesses in Jerusalem and all Judea and Samaria and to the ends (the very bounds) of the earth". (Acts 1:8).

They were simple fishermen on the Galilean lake; men with little or no training or education; men with no position or standing. They were, at best, Jews, and the nation was everywhere scorned, and those peasants were not even men of respect within their own nation. However, by becoming disciples of Jesus, they were given the authority to flip the world upside down.

Jesus Christ forewarned them that, for His account, they would be dragged before rulers and kings and persecuted wherever they went. The Master tasked the disciples to preach the gospel in the midst of Rome's imperial authority, Greece's ancient knowledge, and the savage cruelties of primitive regions and to establish a kingdom of peace and righteousness.

When Jesus handed the disciples their commission, He also told them they would lose His physical presence. They had no fear while He was with them. When the Scribes and Pharisees troubled them at any point, they turned to Jesus who saved them from their uncertainty. Never before had any human spoken like the Man Jesus. Never did wisdom and prudence like His dwell in any mind as they did in His. The disciples' sponsorship was Jesus' presence, the massive umbrella under which they stood safely no matter what shafts their enemies launched at them. But then, as He was leaving the world to return to the Father, they would be without their fortress and high tower. The disciples would be like children without their fathers or, at best, soldiers without a commander. This was a tragic case. Work is assigned, and power is withdrawn: a battle begins, and the conquering commander departs.

Love constantly wishes to be with the object it loves, and its absence creates pain:

"But because I have said these things to you, sorrow has filled your heart [taken complete possession of them]." (John 16:6).

Jesus had become the glory of their eyes, the sun of their days, and the star of their nights: like the husband, they relied on their beloved as she appeared from the wilderness. The disciples were soon about to become like little orphans since their Lord and Master were leaving them. They could have a lot of heartbreak. And when Jesus saw their sorrow, he spoke to them:

"If I go not away, the Comforter will not come unto you; but if I depart, I will send him unto you" (John 16:7 KJV).

The disciples were thrilled when Jesus informed them that His departure would be for their benefit rather than their loss. He told them that when He be gone, the Holy Spirit would come to be their Advocate and Friend.

And with the power of the Holy Spirit, they would be able to suppress all their enemies and finish their work. The Holy Spirit was to be their Teacher and Comforter so they would not be anxious, and their Advocate so they would not be confused. When they talked, a power within them would propose their words. That power, the power of the Holy Spirit who is one God with the Father and the Son, would be divine; the power of those words would convince their hearers and the power in their hearers would cause the Word stated to dwell in their memories.

Ironically, Jesus Christ continually referred to the Holy Spirit as a Person referring to the Spirit as "Him" rather than as an effect, effluence, or anything else that may be described by the impersonal pronoun "it". The Holy Spirit's impact may, thus, be called impersonal, but He, Himself, is presented as a Personality as legitimate as the Father or the Son.

Throughout the Bible, He is depicted as one with the Father and the Son. He has a fundamental relationship with them, and they are completely in agreement on all matters relevant to the betterment of humanity.

Many Christians wonder whether the Holy Spirit was sent alone by the Father or by both the Father and the Son. But, as He was sent by the Father to finish His part of the work of redemption, Jesus Christ asserts that the Holy Spirit is sent by the Father and the Son to continue and complete His part of the work until the world is restored to God.

"However, I am telling you nothing but the truth when I say it is profitable (good, expedient, advantageous) for you that I go away. Because if I do not go away, the Comforter (Counselor, Helper Advocate, intercessor, Strengthener, Standby) will not come to you [to be in close fellowship with you]. And when He comes, He will convict and convince the world and bring demonstration to it about sin and about righteousness (uprightness of heart and right standing with God) and about judgment:" (John 14:7-8).

While performing His share of the redemption work, the Holy Spirit also serves as the Son's (Jesus) Revealer:

"For He will not speak His own message [on His own authority]; but He will tell whatever He hears [from the Father; He will give the message that has been given to Him], and He will announce and declare to you the things that are to come [that will happen in the future]." (John 14:13c).

At the time of Jesus' ascension, only about 500 converts were to show for it. However, by sending the Holy Spirit, Jesus Christ laid the groundwork for His disciples to accomplish greater things. All of the greater work done by the disciples was possible because when Jesus Christ left them, He placed them under the guidance and direction of the Holy Spirit of power and victory.

*"Love constantly wishes to be with
the object it loves, and its
absence creates pain."*

One God, Not Three Gods

Many Christians argue passionately that if the Father is God, the Son is God, and the Holy Spirit is God, then there are three Gods. The dilemma is evident, but how can such Christians get out of it? Humanly speaking, in certain ways, the humanity of Jesus Christ is a bit complex:

"For to us, a Child is born, to us a Son is given; and the government shall be upon His shoulder, and His name shall be called Wonderful Counselor, Mighty God, Everlasting Father [of Eternity], Prince of Peace" (Isaiah 9:6).

In the same sentence, Isaiah refers to Jesus as *"a Child", "a Counselor"* a *"Son"* and *"the Everlasting Father"*. How can Jesus, the Man of Sorrows, also be God overall, blessed forever? How can He, who is usually referred to as the Son in the Divine Trinity, be legitimately referred to as *"the Everlasting Father?"*

Furthermore, during His time on earth, Jesus Christ taught the Divine position of the Father, the Son, and the Holy Spirit. Jesus believed that there is only one God, and He often reiterated this belief, particularly when He encountered the woman of Samaria:

"God is a Spirit (a spiritual Being) and those who worship Him must worship Him in spirit and in truth (reality)." (John 4:24).

As a devout Jew, Jesus was committed to the truth of the Torah which begins: "In the beginning God", and whose fundamental teaching is that there is only one God and that there is none beside Him.

In His response to the scribe about the first commandment of the Ten Commandments, Jesus may have referred to the scribe's frontlet which bore this inscription:

"Jesus answered, The first and principal one of all commands is: Hear, O Israel, The Lord our God is one Lord;" (Mark 12:29).

Throughout His whole teaching, Jesus focused on the Decalogue's legitimacy and the inescapable authority as the great symbol of a moral rule, the cornerstone of which is spelled out in the statement:

"I am the Lord your God, Who has brought you out of the land of Egypt, out of the house of bondage. You shall have no other gods before or besides Me." (Exodus 20:2-3).

So, how can God be one while also being three? That is where the mystery of the unfathomable Trinity is revealed. Despite speaking about the Father, Himself, and the Holy Spirit, Jesus Christ makes no attempt to explain the Trinity anywhere in the Bible. Jesus did not need to explain because just as there are secret agents in the administrations of developed countries, there should be one in the government of God.

A human being is composed of three parts: body, soul, and spirit. However, no one knows how a human's inner spirit is connected to their body. We do not know where the three parts intersect. There is no doctor who understands the linkage between the soul and tendons. We do not know where spirit begins and matter ends. No scientist can explain how the spirit is capable of operating on matter at all. We do not understand how a spirit may inhabit a corporeal home, look through our eyes, listen through our ears, speak through our lips, and execute its will with our hands.

Our noses, ears, eyes, and hands are all made of clay. They are made of the same material that we encounter on the street and playground. It is just earth's soil, wisely shaped materialism by God. Despite corruptible materialism, the soul indwells and inhabits the house of clay — a far more incredible thing than God being three Persons but One. We cannot understand the human Trinity in the same way that we cannot understand the Divine Trinity. And if we refuse to accept what we do not understand, we shall be in mental danger. In truth, we can only ask that the proposition presented to us is not paradoxical.

The Trinity theory is mysterious, but no more so than ten thousand other facts that we accept without question because we cannot ignore them. Let it be enough on its own to say that our Jesus Christ acknowledged the doctrine as true. God is three persons in one essence, Tri-unity, or three in one. That mystifies but does not violate our reasoning, so we can afford to leave the solution to the Godhead:

"Know (perceive, recognize, and understand with approval) that the Lord is God! It is He Who has made us, not we ourselves [and we are His]! We are His people and the sheep of His pasture. Enter into His gates with thanksgiving and a thank offering and into His courts with praise! Be thankful and say so to Him, bless and affectionately praise His name! For the Lord is good; His mercy and loving-kindness are everlasting, His faithfulness and truth endure to all generations." (Psalm 100:3-5).

In His final teachings about the Holy Spirit, Jesus Christ assured His disciples that:

"I have told you these things while I am still with you. But the Comforter (Counselor, Helper, Intercessor, Advocate, Strengthener, Standby), the Holy Spirit, Whom the Father will send in My name [in My place, to represent Me and act on My behalf], He will teach you all things. And He will cause you to recall (will remind you of, bring to your remembrance) everything I have told you." (John 14:26).

It is, therefore, not contradictory, nor is it a dilemma, but it is a miracle that He who was a baby should be infinite at the same time. To avoid confusion with Him who is preeminently known as "THE FATHER", it is important to clarify in conclusion that Jesus (Son) is not the "Father" (God). In respect of the Godhead, Jesus' real name is the Son, not the Father. The Son is not the Father, and the Father is not the Son. They are one God, ultimately and eternally, forever one and indivisible. Nonetheless, the differentiation of the Persons must be carefully acknowledged and respected.

*"We cannot understand the human
Trinity in the same way that
we cannot understand the
Divine Trinity."*

CHAPTER 02

The Virgin Birth

God planned a wonderful birth for the best Who was ever born of a woman.

Mary's pregnancy and birth of Jesus are unprecedented events; they are miraculous and God-like. The narrative of Jesus Christ's miraculous conception is unrivaled in the Bible and throughout history. It is never mentioned of any other woman of virgin birth other than the Virgin Mary. And it is only Jesus Christ who is ever mentioned as having a virgin mother:

"Behold, the virgin shall become pregnant and give birth to a Son, and they shall call His name Emmanuel-which, when translated, means God with us." (Matthew 1:23).

God, from the beginning, had ordained that His Son would be *"born of a woman"*:

"And I will put enmity between you and woman, and between your offspring and her Offspring; He will bruise and tread your head underfoot, and you will lie in wait and bruise His heel." (Genesis 3:15).

And there was peculiar wisdom decreeing that Jesus Christ (Son) should be the son of the woman, not the son of the man. If Jesus had been born of flesh, *"that which is born of flesh is flesh"*, "He would have received all the flaws, sins, and weaknesses that humanity has from (corporeal) birth. He, like the rest of humanity, would have been conceived in sin and fashioned in iniquity:

"Behold, I was brought forth in [a state of] iniquity; my mother was sinful who conceived me [and I too am sinful]."(Psalm 51:5).

As a result, He was not born of man; however, the Holy Spirit overshadowed Mary:

But as he was thinking this over, behold, an angel of the Lord appeared to him in a dream, saying, Joseph, descendant of David, do not be afraid to take Mary [as] your wife, for that which is conceived in her is of (from, out of) the Holy Spirit." (Matthew 1:20).

Thus, Jesus Christ stands as the only Man, except one other (First Adam), who came forth pure from His Maker's hands, and who could ever declare, "I am immaculate". Yes, Jesus could claim much more about His pureness than that other Adam could, for He retained His dignity and never let it go, and from His birth to His death, Jesus knew no sin, nor was deceit found in His tongue.

The birth of Jesus Christ into the world is a pure source of joy. We connect great deep sadness with His crucifixion, yet we derive nothing but joy from His birth in Bethlehem. When the Eternal God descended from heaven and took on the form of His own creature who had rebelled against Him, the action could not be detrimental to humanity. When Matthew talks about the birth of Jesus Christ, he says:

"Now all this was done, that it might be fulfilled which was spoken of the Lord by the prophet, saying, Behold, a virgin shall be with child and shall bring forth a son, and they shall call His name Emmanuel." (Matthew 1:212-23 KJV).

God, in our human nature, is God with us, not God against us. The phrase "God with us!" is a magnificent thrill. "GOD with us!" the Godhead, the eternal Creator with us, is worthy of the dawn song explosion, as angels surprised the shepherds with their songs singing:

"Glory to God in the highest, and on earth peace, goodwill to men." (Luke 2:14 KJV).

The angels' singing of Jesus' birth provided an appropriate background to the celebration. It was the humble fact that resulted in the entire world's being filled with peace and goodwill.

The baby born in Bethlehem was God, and He is "God with us!" God, God, there is glory; "God with us!" there is compassion; — that is majesty; this is grace; that is "God with us!" Any other person, like Simeon, could take the baby Jesus in their arms and feel that they have seen the Lord's salvation; it could not mean harm to them:

[Simeon] too Him up in his arms and praised and thanked God..." (Luke 2:28)

The birth of Jesus Christ was humble. He was not born in a home or a palace. Although being a Prince, He was not dressed in purple but was swaddled in an ordinary cloth in a manger, possibly where the oxen came to feed from the same manger:

"And she gave birth to her Son, her Firstborn; and she wrapped Him in swaddling clothes and laid Him in a manger, because there was no room or place for them in the inn." (Luke 2:7).

The Interrupters Of Jesus' Earthly Mission

Because they had no understanding of the spiritual significance of Jesus' mission, the Pharisees, Priests, Sadducees, Scribes, and others opposed Him in their own harsh and vicious way. No human being has ever been more compassionate, respectful, gracious, and accommodating than Jesus Christ; it is difficult not to love Him. At first glance, it appears to be far more difficult to hate Him than to love Him. Nonetheless, as lovable as Jesus is, "altogether lovely", no human being has ever faced hostility so early or endured such continual persecution as He had.

Jesus Christ was no sooner ushered into the world than the sword of Herod was ready to cut Him off. Because of Jesus, Herod ordered the murder of innocent babies in Bethlehem, a heartbreaking foretaste of the sorrows Jesus Christ would experience and the hatred that humanity would heap on His noble head. Except for a little respite, while Jesus was a child, it was as if the entire world was united against Him, and all of the Scribes, Pharisees, Sadducees, etc., intended to destroy Him. Their hostility manifested itself in various ways; sometimes, openly as when they led Jesus to the summit of the hill and attempted to push Him down headlong:

"And rising up, they pushed and drove Him out of the town, and [laying hold of Him] they led Him to the [projecting] upper part of the hill on which their town was built, that they might hurl Him headlong down [over the cliff]." (Luke 4:29).

On another occasion, they took up stones again to stone Him because He said Abraham wished to see His day, and he saw it and rejoiced:

"Then the Jews said to Him, You are not yet fifty years old, and have You seen Abraham? Jesus replied, I assure you, most solemnly I tell you, before Abraham was born, I Am. So they took up stones to throw at Him, but Jesus, by mixing with the crowd, concealed Himself and went out of the temple [enclosure]." (John 8:57-59).

Other times, their hatred towards Jesus manifested itself in slanderous words.

"The Son of Man has come eating and drinking, and you say, Behold, a Man Who is a glutton and a wine drinker, a friend of tax collectors and notorious sinners. (Luke 7:34).

Other times, their hostility manifested in contemptuous looks, such as when they stared suspiciously at Jesus because He ate with publicans and sinners and sat at the table without washing His hands.

"When the Pharisees saw this, they said to His disciples, Why does your Master eat with tax collectors and those [preeminently] sinful?" (Matthew 9:11).

At times, their hatred consumed them completely, and they thought to themselves:

"And behold, some of the scribes said to themselves, This man blasphemes [He claims the rights and prerogatives of God] But Jesus, knowing (seeing) their thoughts, said, Why do you think evil and harbor malice in your hearts? For which is easier: to say, Your sins are forgiven and the penalty remitted, or to say, Get up and walk?" (Matthew 9:3-5).

Jesus Christ's earthly public ministry was a home mission. Hence, He told His disciples:

"He answered, I was sent only to the lost of the house of Israel." (Matthew 15:24).

Jesus Christ began His mission as His great instrument preaching the gospel with a great home mission. God had anointed Him to preach the gospel. He performed thousands of gracious acts; He served in a variety of capacities for the benefit of His fellow humans and the glory of God.

As a beloved Son and Prince of Heaven, Jesus' earthly throne was definitely the pulpit. His full glory was revealed when He began to proclaim the gospel of the kingdom of God.

"The attendants replied, Never has a man talked as this Man talks! [No mere man has ever spoken as He speaks!]" (John 7:46).

Jesus traveled to the very borders of the Holy Land, but He stayed and preached to His own people north and south, east and west, in all areas, in towns and villages. In His home mission, Jesus Christ still had two major goals in mind for His ministry. The first was to preach the gospel to the distant masses in order to gather a group of disciples for Himself from among them. He continued with great zeal and perseverance for the first portion of His mission traveling the Holy Land from end to end and meeting people here and there, but never ceased to proclaim the gospel to the multitude that gathered to Him.

His second objective was to train those who became His disciples so that having gathered them to Himself, He might teach them the truth. He gathered twelve different people from different locations, times, and backgrounds and unified them as one body calling them His disciples. He taught them about the Father and His love, Himself, His work, His death, and His resurrection. He also, on many occasions, taught them about the Holy Spirit as the Divine Comforter and His indwelling, as well as everything else that would benefit their spiritual growth and profit. In connection with Jesus' own personal teaching of His disciples, we find His forming prenatal care.

For three years and above, Jesus Christ taught His disciples with words and deeds perfumed with love. His words were constantly evolving, and the Holy Spirit was present in every utterance. That heavenly Spirit was deeply infused and impregnated into each letter. So, Jesus' disciples, as they listened to Him every day, became much more impregnated with the Holy Spirit. The words from Jesus' lips overshadowed the disciples and impregnated them like the Holy Spirit that overshadowed Mary to impregnate her.

And so, for three and half years, they carried the words of Jesus in their wombs. In the beginning, when God created the world, it was a chaotic mass of substance with no order. Yet, God the Holy Spirit spread His wings over it and sowed the seeds of life in it; He deposited the seeds from which all creatures grew; He nourished the earth so that it could sustain life. In the same way, Jesus partnered with the Holy Spirit to hover over this world through the disciples in order to create order out of the chaos that was the status of the world during His time. And after that, what is known as the foreign mission arose from Jesus Christ and the Holy Spirit homework got approved by the Father when the disciples who were scattered abroad traveled and preached the gospel everywhere, and thus, the blessing of Israel became the blessing of all humanity.

The disciples of Jesus were, therefore, impregnated with "the gospel" and the "Holy Spirit" anticipating their delivery day like a pregnant woman anticipates her delivery day.

When Man Became A Devil Man

Man did to Jesus Christ what we sometimes do to one another. They became deicides and slew God. They nailed God on the cross. The death of Jesus Christ is a solemn decree of God fulfilled by men who were the ignorant but guilty instruments of its accomplishment.

It was appointed that Jesus Christ must die. But He was not to die in a vehicle or a plane crash. An accidental death would withdraw the necessary bitterness from His cup making it wormwood mingled with gall. He was not to be captured during a world war. No such death would have depicted Jesus Christ as an unwilling victim. He did not become a fugitive where His national Interpol were to hunt for Him. Such an incident would not have rendered His death a sacrifice. And if He had offered Himself to His captors, they would have exonerated themselves from being the initial culprits. They would have made Him a party to their crime.

The rightful way the Godhead appointed Jesus Christ to die was through a betrayal by His friend. Death by the betrayal of a friend made Jesus Christ bear the utmost depths of suffering. And surely, there was a well of grief in every separate circumstance in His death. When Satan, the master abuser, had been entirely conquered in his conflict with Jesus Christ in the Garden, the man-devil Judas came upon the scene. Judas became Satan's deputy abuser, a proxy abuser, and the most trusty and serviceable tool. The master abuser took the entire possession of his deputy's heart. It was well calculated that the abuser would choose one of Jesus Christ's personal friends to be His treacherous deceiver. Because in doing so, Satan was able to stab Jesus Christ right in His heart.

Beyond a doubt, however, the main reason for Jesus Christ to be betrayed by a friend was for Him to offer a perfect atonement for sin. We may usually read the sin in the punishment. Adam, the federal head of the human race, betrayed God in the Garden of Eden. He had custody of the royal Garden and should have kept its green avenues sacred for communion with his God. But Adam betrayed the trust; the sentinel was false; he admitted evil into his heart and the paradise of God. Adam betrayed the good name of the Creator by accepting the sarcastic words that he ought to have dismissed with contempt.

Therefore, just as Satan used a serpent to convince a man to betray God's trust, it was necessary for him to use a man to betray Jesus Christ. There must be a counterpart of the sin in the suffering which He endured.

The murder of Jesus Christ was the extreme of human abuse. It developed the deadly hatred against God lurking in Man's heart. When man became a deicide, abuse reached its fullness. That fullness was displayed in the black deed of the man by whom Jesus Christ was betrayed. Judas and all his cohorts serve as a stark example of how abusive human nature has become.

"When Man became a deicide, abuse reached its fullness."

God Became Man

As the pendulum of the clock continues to beat unceasingly like the heart of time; as morning dawn gives way to evening shade; and the seasons follow in a constant cycle; so does an unbroken abuse. It drifts its victims along the river of shame, pain, lack, and sometimes nearer to death.

Jesus Christ underwent a long cycle of abuse. He was tried before the ecclesiastical and civil tribunals and before the great democratic tribunal: the assembly of the people on the street. He was greatly depressed. The agony of the night in Gethsemane reduced Jesus to a state of extreme weakness. He was scourged and cruelly mocked all through the morning: from Annas, Caiaphas, Pilate, Herod, and the Praetorian guards.

For five times in cycles, the soldiers took Jesus Christ back and forth and mocked Him. They continuously spat upon Him and treated Him shamefully. Nonetheless, neither the weakness of the past nor the agony of the present could stop the executioners, the four soldiers at Golgotha, from abusing Him.

If you have an averagely compassionate heart, you will feel the urge to console someone when you encounter them in tremendous sorrow. Unfortunately, abuse spreads easily. It has some kind of hidden ability to distort humanity's basic compassion. Abuse has a dreadful contagious, and infectious quality wherever it manifests.

Hence, the brutal treatment that Jesus Christ received at the hands of the governor, Praetorian guards, and all of the priests caused the four soldiers to lose all sense of humanity and sympathy for Him. Undoubtedly, the more misery and shame the four soldiers inflicted upon Jesus Christ, the happier they became. Suffice it to say that the death of Jesus Christ was preordained by God. Anyone who reads about Jesus Christ's life and death as a mere history will make a great mistake. They will be tempted to attribute all of the abuses and injustices He suffered to Jewish hostility, the priests' erratic behavior, and Pilate's political misconduct.

God is not simply a spectator to salvation. He showed the world His sovereign Fatherly love by sending His Son, Jesus Christ, into the world. God Himself came to the world in the Person of Jesus Christ, paying a special visit to Jerusalem and the Jewish people. Through that visitation, God has come near to the rest of humanity.

God, the Compassionate Architect of salvation, has the software that designed salvation entirely in His power. In that designed software, there is nothing drawn by a stranger's hand. The penmanship of the solemn software of salvation is, from beginning to end, entirely divine.

Therefore, the mystery surrounding Jesus Christ's crucifixion is more than just Jewish or Roman malice or abuse. It was the solemn command of God carried out by them. It is true that they were justified in all of their abusive behaviors toward Jesus Christ. However, those who turned into deicides by abusing God and crucifying Him must bear responsibility for the crime and repent.

Jesus Christ's death was extraordinarily complex. It was both good and bad: He had to die to save sinners, but He did so at the hands of the guilty but ignorant accomplices. Now, let us go back to the theme of the four abusive soldiers with Jesus Christ at Golgotha. In the type of the Passover lamb in the Old Testament, it was expressly enacted that not a bone of it should be broken "... *neither shall you break a bone of it"* (Exodus 12:46c). Therefore, the soldiers did not have a bone of Jesus Christ. However, to fulfill the prophecy, He was to be pierced with the nails.

"But one of the soldiers pierced His side with a spear, and immediately blood and water came (flowed) out." (John 19:34).

Jesus Christ, for a while, endured a lot of pain. He was at Golgotha, and the four soldiers were evidently determined to carry out the governor's orders. The soldiers had commenced their dreadful task. Jesus Christ had undergone His first pain of crucifixion; the soldiers had then driven the nails through His hands and feet. The crosses had then been arranged so that Jesus was hanging in the midst of two criminals. He was the second of the three. The soldiers had broken the legs of the first criminal. Naturally, the soldiers were to proceed to Jesus Christ. But they seemed to pass by Him on the second cross and proceeded from the first to the third. The soldier did not break His legs. It would have been most gratifying to see the soldiers cease such loathsome brutality. That gladness would have been short-lived; for the soldier had to commit another outrage. To make sure that Jesus Christ was dead, one of the four soldiers with a spear pierced His side, probably thrusting His lance quite through the heart.

"But one of the soldiers pierced His side with a spear, and immediately blood and water came (flowed) out." (John 19:34).

The four Roman soldiers were keen executioners in what they were ordered to do. And they saw to it that *"He was dead already."*

"But when they came to Jesus and they saw that He was already dead, they did not break His legs." (John 19:33).

The soldiers, with their spears, made Jesus Christ's death a certainty. From the behavior of the four soldiers, it did not seem at all likely that when they were ordered to break the legs of the crucified Jesus, they were going to abstain from breaking Jesus Christ's legs. If an abusive soldier would spare Jesus Christ's bones, why would he not also spare His flesh but would nail and pierce His side? How could those soldiers keep away from one act of violence, and which was apparently authorized for execution and yet, perpetrated another violence which had not been suggested to them? But, let the case be as complicated as it was possible for it to have been; Infinite Wisdom knew how to work it out in all points. And It did perfectly so.

There are prophecies about Jesus Christ and about everything connected with Him. From His birth to His ministry to His tomb: everything about the prophecy had to be carried out to the letter. Nobody but God, the Great Architect, has the singular mandate to determine how prophecies, which are of all kinds and appear to be confused and even in contradiction to one another, must be fulfilled. Jesus Christ is the exact substance of the foreshadowing of the Messianic prophecies. The cycle of Jesus Christ's abusers was far-reaching, which included Herod the great, the Scribes and Pharisees, the Sanhedrin, Judas, Annas, Caiaphas, Pilate, Herod the Antipas, the crowd, the ungrateful Jews and the Gentiles — the whole human race in a certain sense committed the brutal abuse of fastening Him to the accursed tree.

"As the pendulum of the clock continues to beat unceasingly like the heart of time; as morning dawn gives way to evening shade; and the seasons follow in a constant cycle; so does an unbroken abuse. It drifts its victims along the river of shame, pain, lack, and sometimes nearer to death."

Man Of Sorrow

The phrase "Man of Sorrow" used in the Bible to describe Jesus Christ is meant to be extremely emphatic. Clearly, He was not "a sorrowful man" because He was noted to be going about His work joyfully in spite of all the troubles involved. "Man of sorrow" could mean Jesus Christ was essentially composed of sorrows; they formed a fundamental part of whom He was.

Many people may not know their real names. They may know the names their parents gave them during their naming. They may know the names and titles which people use in addressing them. But they may not know the names people use when speaking of them. But Jesus Christ knew His name. He must have requested a name change from Jesus to Sorrow so that those who saw Him would see sorrow, and those seeking sorrow would simply look for Him.

No person in the human race is completely unaffected by sorrow. You will experience sorrow whether you live on land, in the sky, or in the sea.

Alas! Mothers soon lose their children, and husbands and wives lose the ones they love the most! No human being, born to a woman, does not experience the thorns and thistles that we inherited from Adam. Jesus Christ is called "Man of sorrow" by way of prominence. He was not simply sorrowful but pre-eminent among the sorrowful.

There is almost some ancientness to every story in the world. Most people deal with people after the latest news. But it is usually wise to go back to the earliest records. Physicians who know what they are doing ask more about their patient's history. It does us good to look back upon why Jesus Christ, also God, was dubbed "Man of Sorrow."

His birth was so joyful that the angel who came to announce it was overcome with joy. The angel's bosom was filled with a sweet benevolence of Spirit which made him happy. The angel had such gladsome tidings to bring to the fallen sons of men. As it was where he came from, the angel happily conveyed his message. The theme which brought him down and his own interest therein was captured in the message:

"I bring you good tidings of great joy." (Luke 1:19 KJV).

We are sure he spoke in accents of delight. The angels were so glad at the gospel. When the discourse was over, with one angel having evangelized and given out the gospel for the day, a band of choristers suddenly appeared. A great number of the heavenly host had heard that a chosen messenger had been sent to announce the birth of the King. They were overcome by holy joy and adoration. They gathered their courage to pursue him. They could not let him go to earth alone on such an important mission. They overtook him just as he had reached the last word of his discourse. They burst forth in that famous chorale, the only one sung by angels that human ears had ever heard here below:

"Glory to God in the highest [heaven], and on earth peace among men with whom He is well pleased [men of goodwill, of His favor]." (Luke 2:14).

Alas, Jesus Christ endured persecution from birth. Everything about Him became sorrowful as a result of the human race's sin. It reduced His wealth to poverty. His joy has turned to sorrow, and His glory has turned to shame. However, God compensated His sorrows with glories.

Now come with me to Gethsemane, the place of Jesus Christ's peaceful retirement - the Garden where, in hallowed devotion, He most neared heaven in communion with God. Alas, our sin transformed into the focus of His sorrow, the center of His woe!

*"Abuse has a dreadful contagious,
and infectious quality wherever
it manifests."*

GETHSEMANE

A few of the disciples shared in the sorrow at Gethsemane. The vast majority of them were absent. They lacked the necessary level of grace to be permitted to view the secrets of "the sorrow". The walls of Gethsemane are a suitable metaphor for the lack of grace that effectively shields the more profound wonders of communion from the view of all. Eight of the eleven were left off in the distance. They were disciples, but not in the intimate way that only deeply loved ones are allowed. Peter, James, and John were given the opportunity to enter Gethsemane and observe that very spectacular sight.

As was previously stated, not all of the disciples were given the opportunity to see firsthand the sorrow that Jesus Christ underwent in the place of the olive press – the moments when the higher and lower millstones of mental anguish and infernal cruelty buried Him. Therefore, it is evidently beyond anyone's ability to explain it to one another. All must have access to the wonders of

Gethsemane through Jesus Himself. It is God's wish that everyone would come into the Garden.

The Son Of God At Gethsemane

The Bible employs a lot of phrases to describe Jesus Christ's emotions leading to the Dolorous night. Matthew writes of Jesus Christ: *"He began to be sorrowful and sore troubled."* It is translated *"very heavy"*. John described Jesus Christ days before as: *"Now is my soul troubled"*. As He marked the gathering clouds He hardly knew where to turn Himself, and cried out: "What shall I say?" Every statement made by Jesus Christ demonstrates that He was disturbed during His ordeal:

"My soul is exceeding sorrowful even unto death". (Matt 26:38 KJV).

Jesus' peace became a powerful storm, and His calm disappeared. The intensity of His anguish nearly drove the beloved of the Father to panic. Throughout His life, Jesus Christ scarcely uttered an expression of grief. Yet, in Gethsemane, Jesus Christ spoke not only through His sighs and bloody sweat, but also through so many words: "My soul is exceeding sorrowful oven unto death".

Jesus Christ could not conceal His grief. He did not appear to want to do so. He ran backwards and forwards three times to His disciples. He allowed them to see His sorrow and appealed to them for sympathy. His exclamations were piteous, and His sighs and groans were probably terrible to hear. He said it all when He described His Soul as *"My soul is exceeding sorrowful, even unto death"*. He meant He was enveloped in sorrow and surrounded by it. He meant He had no breathing holes and that His entire body was drenched in sorrow. His struggles meant when He tried to free

Himself from the sticky, thick sorrow; He dropped farther and further since He had neither a handhold nor a foothold.

It was not an aching of the brow; it was worse than that. The trouble of the Spirit is worse than the pain of the body. Pain in the body can cause problems and be an unintentional source of grief. But how well can a man bear pain if their mind is perfectly clear? When the soul is exhilarated and lifted up with inward joy after conquering the body, the pain of the body is almost forgotten.

On the other hand, the soul's sorrow created bodily pain; the lower nature sympathized with the higher. Our outward appearance is usually the index of our mind. There is always sympathy between body and soul. And the main source of Jesus Christ's suffering was in His soul—His soul-sufferings were the soul of His sufferings. The pain of the Spirit is the worst of pain; the sorrow of the heart is the climax of grief.

Jesus Christ's sorrow of heart led to a very deep depression of His Spirit, *"very heavy"*. The Son of God was depressed; it was not pain or a palpitation of the heart. The word "heavy" has a lot of meaning — more meaning than it is easy to explain. And the root of the words Jesus Christ employed signifies He was *"separated from the people — men in distraction, being separated from mankind"*. The original word is extremely difficult to translate. It could represent mental abstraction. It's completely consumed by grief, to the exclusion of any thought that could have alleviated the pain. One burning thought consumed His entire soul consuming everything that could have provided comfort.

For a time, Jesus Christ's mind refused to consider the outcome of His death. The subsequent joy that was set before Him. His position as a sin bearer, and the subsequent abandonment by His Father, absorbed His thoughts and hurried His soul away from everything else. Some translate the word to a measure of distraction. It appears Jesus Christ's mind underwent perturbations and convulsions widely different from His usual calm and collected Spirit. He was tossed back and forth like a mighty sea of trouble, wrought to tempest. In its rage, it carried Him away.

"Surely He has borne our griefs (sicknesses, weaknesses, and distresses) and carried our sorrows and pains [of punishment], yet we [ignorantly] considered Him stricken, smitten, and afflicted by God [as if with leprosy]." (Isaiah 53:4).

With overwhelming despair, Jesus Christ's heart melted like wax in the midst of His bowels. He was described as "very heavy". Some believe the word means "separated from the people" at its root as if Jesus Christ evolved into a unique human being. He was as if his mind had been jolted by a sudden blow or pressed by some incredible calamity. He was no more as ordinary men are. Mere onlookers would have thought of Him as a distraught man, burdened beyond the wont of men. He was borne down by a sorrow unparalleled among men. Thomas Goodwin says: "very heavy" denotes *"a failing, a deficiency, and a sinking of Spirit. It is a kind such as happens to people in sickness and swounding".*

Bloody perspiration was the primary way that Jesus Christ's sorrow was revealed. Jesus Christ's soul was ill and disoriented as if He was ill with Epaphroditus' illness which brought Him dangerously close to death. The bloody sweat was a very unusual phenomenon. Never in Jesus Christ's life did He sweat blood. Only in the final grim struggle among the olive trees did He resist unto blood agonizing over sin. Jesus Christ was a Man in good health; He was only thirty-three years of age. However, the mental strain brought on by His attempt to focusing on what lay ahead of Him was inexplicable. As He used all of His might to focus on it, His body got so aroused that large drops of blood began to flow from His pores and fall to the ground. Jesus Christ's sweat was produced by exhaustion. The cold, sweaty sweat of dying men is caused by body faintness. But Jesus' bloody sweat came from utter faintness and soul prostration. He was in a terrible soul-swoon and died inwardly with no accompanying watery tears from the eyes. Jesus Christ's sweating was a weeping of blood from the entire man.

"The trouble of the Spirit is worse than the pain of the body."

JUDAS, A CLOSE CONFIDANT OF JESUS CHRIST

Judas was Jesus Christ's servant, maybe, His confidential servant. He was a partaker in the apostolic ministry and in the honor of miraculous gifts. Judas was a preacher; he was a foremost preacher, and *"He obtained part of this ministry"* (Acts 1:25). Doubtlessly, Judas had preached the gospel and many had been gladdened by his voice. Maybe, Jesus Christ had vouchsafed to Him special miraculous powers so that at his word, the sick got healed. Perhaps, by his ministry, deaf ears opened, and the blind were made to see. There is no doubt Judas was not simply one of the seventy. He had been selected by Jesus Christ as one of the twelve. Hence, he was an honorable member of the college of the apostles. I believe Judas, who, in the end, made his heart an abode for abuse, might have cast abusive spirits out of others.

Jesus Christ and the disciples treated Judas Iscariot most kindly and indulgently. He had food and raiment given him out of the common stock. Jesus Christ seemed to have indulged Judas very greatly. John claimed He was the beloved disciple (John 13:23 KJV). However, it is safe to say Judas Iscariot was also close to Jesus Christ by virtue of His position.

With utmost confidence and unlimited trust, Jesus Christ appointed Judas, the treasurer of the disciples. Jesus Christ committed into Judas' hands the little bag into which generous women cast their small contributions. And very wisely, too, he had the financial vein. His main virtue was economy, a very needful quality in a treasurer, as exercising a prudent foresight for the little disciples' company and watching the expenses carefully. He was, as far as men could judge, the right man in the right place. Jesus Christ had thoroughly trusted him. It was not recorded in the Bible that there was any annual audit of Judas' accounts; I do not discover that the Master took him to task as to the expenditure of his privy purse. Everything was given to Judas, and he gave, at Jesus Christ's direction, to the poor, but no one audited his account.

A Betrayal With A Kiss

Jesus Christ had been much in prayer. Through prayer, Jesus Christ overcame His dreadful agitation. He was very calm and gentle even when He was forsaken by a friend. Judas betrayed Jesus Christ with a kiss:

"And he came up to Jesus at once and said, Hail (greetings, good health to You, long life to You), Master! And he embraced Him and kissed Him with [pretended] warmth and devotion" (Matthew 26:49).

Jesus Christ did not refer to Judas with any derogatory titles. He did not use any hurtful remarks toward Judas. Jesus Christ was very amiable.

If there was anything godly left in Judas, Jesus Christ's response to him would have brought it out.

"Friend, for what are you here? Then they came up and laid hands-on Jesus and arrested Him" (Matthew 26:50).

Jesus Christ asked Judas:

"But Jesus said to him, Judas! Would you betray and deliver up the Son of Man with a kiss?" (Luke 22:48).

If Judas had not been an unmitigated, incorrigible, thrice-dyed abuser, his avarice must have lost its power at that instant. Judas would have cried:

"My Lord! I came to betray You, but Your generous response has won my soul. I give myself up to be bound instead of You".

Judas would have fully confessed his infamy.

Jesus Christ also referred to Judas' act as a betrayal. He had a reproof in them, but He still was kind and good towards such a caitiff. Jesus Christ's eyes may have been welled up with tears and His voice, apparently, may have faltered when He addressed His own familiar friend and acquaintance. Jesus Christ asked:

"Judas my disciple, do you betray me? Judas my treasurer, Judas my colleague and partner do you betray me?"

National Ingratitude

The abuse of the Jews of Jesus Christ's day was a gross act of ingratitude. It was superlative kindness which brought Jesus Christ to that nation in particular and to the sons of men in general: it was supreme ingratitude when that nation, alas, in this, representing us all, would not receive Him but would choose Barabbas over Jesus Christ. The Jews were a favored people above all nations. It was a distinguishing mark of divine favor that Jesus Christ should be born among them. They ought to have appreciated Him with delight. His signs and evidence of Messiahship were clear enough. Jesus Christ wrought among them unprecedented miracles. He spoke as none other man spoke: yet, they chanted: *"Crucify Him"*. The Jews treated their best friend like He had been their worst foe. This was a high-handed act of national abuse.

Many of the people of Israel became partakers of Jesus Christ's healing power. He opened many eyes giving them blessed light. He caused sound to enter many deaf ears. At His bidding, He caused many lame people to leap like a hart. Many people that were sick of palsy and all manner of diseases were suddenly restored by His Word.

Jesus Christ fed thousands of hungry people. He multiplied loaves and fish and fed crowds so that they all ate and were filled. He practically went about *"Doing good"*. His journey was not one of an aimless wandering here and there and everywhere — *"He went about doing good"*.

Jesus Christ preached good tidings to the meek and opened the prisons to them that were bound. Even the gates of death were no match for His goodness' errands. When her son was restored, the widow at the gate of Nain felt her heart leap within her. Mary and Martha were glad when Jesus Christ resurrected Lazarus from his grave. He spent His whole life for humanity. He lived first for God's glory and for the love of men. His meat and drink were to do good to men. He forgot Himself; He utterly renounced all ambitious purposes. Jesus Christ gave Himself away so that He might seek and save the lost. As a mother devotes herself to her babe, so did He lay Himself out for humanity. Jesus Christ loved every human being in the world. However, continually, in every way, men sought to take away His life. His life was a life that was more valuable to them than it was to Him. It was for mankind's sake only that He continued still to live on earth. Many times, He had to escape human's cruel hands. And when He came, humanity was so eager to conspire to hound Him to His death.

For a time, Jesus Christ was very popular with the Jews, as anyone would be who had loaves and fish to distribute. Yet, those people did not have affection for His person or doctrine. They followed Him simply and alone for what they could get from Him. Many of those selfish followers, doubtlessly, gave their voices against Jesus Christ and shouted, "Crucify Him! Crucify Him!". They ate bread with Him but lifted up their heel against Him.

One would have thought when the mob stood in the street of Jerusalem howling out: *"Crucify Him! Crucify Him!"*; Jesus Christ would have been a common informer who had betrayed men for pelf; or maybe a poisoner who had secretly tainted the bread of the people with a deadly drug; or a blasphemer who had profaned every holy thing; or a wretch whose character was doubly dyed in infamy. Instead of that, there stood before that furious crowd the meekest among men. Jesus Christ is the most inoffensive. He is the most generous, the most self-denying, the most tender Man of all of those that were born of a woman. Yet, lustily the crowd cried: *"Crucify Him! Crucify Him!"* When Pilate, the Roman governor, asked the priest: *"Why, what evil hath he done?"* they could give no answer to it, and, therefore, they drowned the question with their shouts: *"Crucify Him! Crucify Him!"* How base an ingratitude of humanity it is to recompense such a life as Jesus Christ with a cruel death!

"The Jews treated their best friend like He had been their worst foe."

THE BACHELOR, THE BACHELORETTE, AND THE CHILD

The Church universal, in whose bosom dwell all Christians, is the bride, the wife of Jesus Christ. The church was both born of Jesus Christ and wedded to Him. In the beginning, God saw that it was not perfect for Adam to live alone. He could not generate his race alone. Therefore, God put a deep sleep upon Adam, took a rib from his side, and formed a woman, Eve, who became Adam's wife. By and through Eve, Adam's wife, he generated his race. Adam could not have brought forth his children in his images of himself without Eve. What do I mean? For a long season before the coming of Jesus Christ, the church was desolate. Her sons and daughters were few. Her solemn feast days were attended by a swarm of hypocrites, and her courts were packed with formalists. But there were sadly few genuine Israelite children. When Jesus

Christ, the Husband of the Church, arrived, the church was in no happy condition. The children of the betrothed wife were but very, very few. At home in heaven, God asked who He could send to redeem the fallen world.

"Also, I heard the voice of the Lord, saying, whom shall I send? And who will go for Us? Then said I, here am I; send me" (Isaiah 6:8).

Without hesitation, Jesus Christ, the Son, advanced to the burning throne and took the book out of the right hand of God who sat upon it. Jesus Christ did not count it robbery to be equal with God. He is *"the very God of the very God"*.

"Who, although being essentially one with God and in the form of God [possessing the fullness of the attributes which make God God], did not think this equality with God was a thing to be eagerly grasped or retained..." (Philippians 2:6).

When Jesus Christ advanced to the throne, He took the book and communed with His Father. He accepted the divine challenge of love and unsealed the mysterious purposes of His Father. To Jesus Christ, there was no danger in a close approach to the infinite glory. That glory was His.

For such an obedience act to His Father, God, the Father, was delighted to honor Jesus Christ, His Only-begotten Son. The Father adores His Son, of whom He is one. The Son has earned favor from the Father. He has been *"obedient unto death, even the death of the cross"*. The Father's goal in the work of grace is to glorify His Son who is the channel of grace to fallen men as God and Man in one nature. Therefore, God proposes to honor Jesus Christ by letting Him to take the church into a marriage union.

But first, according to custom, there had to be a betrothal. Jesus Christ, the Mediator, God and man in one person, together with His Father, decided on the day of the betrothal. On the set day, Jesus Christ manifested. He must come out of the ivory palaces wherein He dwelt. He who was greater than the greatest and higher than the highest fell below the lowest. He did that so that He might save to the uttermost those who come to God by Him.

"Therefore, He is able also to save to the uttermost (completely, perfectly, finally, and for all time and eternity) those who come to God through Him, since He is always living to make petition to God and intercede with Him and intervene for them" (Hebrews 7:25)".

He who is God of all stooped under all the load and burden of sin and became obedient unto death.

"And after He had appeared in human form, He abased and humbled Himself [still further] and carried His obedience to the extreme of death, even the death of the cross!" (Phil. 2:8).

As an eligible Bachelor, Jesus Christ, on the cross, had paid all the customary rites God required to honor Him with the wife. So, God caused Jesus Christ to sleep a deep sleep of death on the cross. And when the soldier pierced Jesus Christ's side, God, apparently, took His rib and formed the church. As a result, the church, like Eve, is Jesus Christ's Bride, *the bone of His bone and flesh of His flesh.*

The identification is more complete if I add one more remark. The church, as a Bride, is also a Mother. The church is the Mother of Jesus Christ's children, but first, she had to be given birth by Jesus Christ in the waters of baptism and by the blood of redemption. One of life's profound mysteries is birth. The Bible regularly uses birth as one of the most visual images of a somber mystery. Instead of pretending to be a physician and delineating every aspect of childbirth, I want to emphasize a relevant point in my scenario. A pregnant woman may occasionally go through a phase known as Braxton Hicks contractions. She may suffer painful contractions in the latter few months of her pregnancy, indicating that her uterus is tightening and relaxing. The woman's membranes also burst at the start or during childbirth. A phenomenon commonly referred to as water breaking. And when the mother ultimately gives birth to the baby, whether naturally or by a cesarean section, she experiences lochia. At that point, the woman begins to bleed normally. That is how her body gets rid of the extra blood and tissue that helped her uterus grow her baby.

When the soldiers pierced Jesus Christ's side, there flowed there out blood and water, upon which a great deal has been said by those who think it proper to dilate upon such tender themes. Some supposed that by death, the blood was divided, and the clots parted from the water in which they floated in a perfectly natural way. But it is not true that blood would flow from a dead body if it were pierced. Only under certain very special conditions would blood gush forth. It is impossible to think of Jesus Christ's side gushing blood as an everyday occurrence—it was a fact in and of itself. I want to use childbirth as the sole piece of evidence in my case because it is well-known.

In the case of Jesus Christ, water and blood naturally flowed from His holy, perfect body. Whether or not it was a miracle, it was undoubtedly a noteworthy and amazing event that Jesus Christ gave birth to the church in the same way a woman gave birth to a child. Jesus Christ's birthing of the church also signifies the new birth everyone is to receive when we come to Him. The Christian is reborn and receives a new nature, an incorruptible seed: God's Word, which has been imbued with our life and quickens us through the Spirit.

*"As an eligible Bachelor,
Jesus Christ, on the cross, had paid
all the customary rites God
required to honor Him with the wife."*

CHAPTER 03

JESUS CHRIST'S PROCESSION

The royal wedding of Prince Charles and Lady Diana Spencer at St. Paul's Cathedral on July 29, 1981, was so lavish that it earned the nickname *"The Wedding of the Century."* The wedding set worldwide fashion trends, broke records, and broke with convention in novel ways. The wedding guest list was a very long one, but it was not with drama. Although every European leader was invited, several chose not to go. To mention but one, due to disagreements over the status of Northern Ireland, the president of the Republic of Ireland declined his invitation. First Lady Nancy Reagan honored her invitation to represent the United States. In the days preceding the big event, the press covered what the world's leaders wore, who they spoke to, and where they partied in London.

Around the world, 750 million people watched the wedding that was aired in 74 nations. The UK made it a national holiday so that more royal citizens could watch the wedding. And Americans set their alarm clocks early to tune in live. More than 600,000 spectators crowded London's streets in an effort to seeing the Prince and the Princess of Wales. One of the most common human impulses is to want to see the person whom everyone loves so much.

Similarly, in Jerusalem, people came out to catch a glimpse of the wedding of all times between Jesus Christ and His bride. To continue with their abusive act on Jesus Christ when He had been condemned to die, the executioners hurried with His sentence. The Jews were in great haste to shed His blood. The enmity of the chief priests and Pharisees was so intense that every moment of delay was wearisome to them. Also, it was the day of the Passover, and they wished to have the matter of Jesus Christ's death finished before they go with hypocritical piety to celebrate the festival of Israel's deliverance.

In all civilized countries, there is usually an interval between the sentencing of the prisoner and the time of their putting to death. Raymond Riles has been on death row for more than 45 years for fatally shooting John Thomas Henry in a Houston car lot in 1974 after a disagreement over a vehicle. As the capital sentence is irreversible, it is well to have a little space in which possible evidence may be forthcoming, which may prevent the fatal stroke. With the Romans, it was usual to allow a reasonable respite of ten days. But jealousy, cruelty, and abuse drove the priest to hasten Jesus Christ's crucifixion. Little did Jesus Christ's abuser know that the crucifixion was a wedding procession for Him and His Bride.

Just as it happened on the streets of London, the Jerusalemites and people from all nations congregated around their windows to watch the Prince of God and His Bride ride through the streets. The crowd, both great and mean men clustered around and beheld only a Bridegroom without a Bride. What a shameful wedding procession! So, all eyes gathered about the Person of Jesus Christ, the Bridegroom.

From heaven, God, the Father, watched each movement of His suffering Son.

The angels watched Him with wonder and amazement. The spirits of the Saints in heaven looked down from heaven's windows on the scene. One of the spectators may be asking: *"Where is the Bride of the Bridegroom?"* Of course, the Bride of Jesus Christ is the Church. And she is invisible to Him. Jesus Christ's Bride was Simon the Cyrene, bearing the cross. The Bride was in the women who were weeping and lamenting.

On July 29, 1981, Prince Charles was with his bride Princess Diana after the nuptials rode in a 1902 State Landau carriage. They wore their royal robes and traversed the streets of London and then to Buckingham Palace.

Jesus Christ, when He was condemned to die, was given over to the brutal soldiers who garrisoned Jerusalem. When they brought Jesus Christ into the guard room, they felt that He was entirely in their power.

To the soldiers, Jesus Christ's claims to be a king were so ridiculous that they could only serve as the subject of mocking satire. They despised Him, the Heir of all things. They bedecked His body with a faded purple robe. And they put a poor reed into His hand for a scepter. The vulgar soldiers then dared to look Jesus Christ in the eyes and worry Him with their filthy jokes as alluded to in Isaiah 53:3:

"He was despised and rejected and forsaken by men, a Man of sorrows and pains, and acquainted with grief..."

Nevertheless, when Jesus Christ began His procession on the Jerusalem streets, the soldiers had taken off the purple from Him and put on Him His own clothes and a crown

"And they dressed Him in [a] purple [robe], and, weaving together a crown of thorns, they placed it on Him" (Mark 15:17).

The soldiery had the power to put Jesus Christ's own clothes upon Him because they were the perquisites of the executioner. In many countries, modern executioners take the garments of those whom they execute. In like manner, the soldiers had the right to Jesus Christ's raiment. They put on Him His own clothes so that the multitudes might recognize Him. Police officers may confirm that people can be completely misled about the identity of individuals. A slight change in clothing, hair color, or jacket color can completely catch a witness off guard. Hence, it was important for Jesus Christ to wear His own cloth; the crowd on the street saw Him as the very Man who had professed to be the Messiah.

The soldiers scornfully put on Jesus Christ's head a crown surrounded with thorns. It was probable that He processed the streets of Jerusalem wearing the crown of thorns along the Via Dolorosa. Yes, He wore the crown to the cross and on the cross. Hence, Pilate wrote upon his accusation: "…the King of the Jews…" (Matt 27:37).

Prince Charles and Princess Diana were surrounded by a multitude of friends. Hark, how they joyously welcomed them! The son of such noble parents deserved a nation's love. But the Prince of Peace was abused without a cause. Hark, how their loud voices demanded that Jesus Christ should be hastened to be executed! How harshly grate the cruel syllables: *"Crucify Him! Crucify Him!"*

Aw, Jesus Christ and His Bride on Good Friday were surrounded by a throng who shouted aloud. They were a multitude who gazed with profound interest. But their disparity was vast. The most careless eye discerned it. Yonder young Prince was ruddy with the bloom of early youth and health. Jesus Christ's visage was more marred than that of any man. His face was blackened with bruises and stained with the shameful spittle of them that derided Him.

Prince Charles and Princess Diana were magnificently driven along the streets of London in a stately chariot sitting at their ease.

Prince Charles and Princes Diana headed on to their honeymoon. Alas, Jesus Christ was being hastened to His doom. The Prince of Peace, the sufferer, walked with weary feet. Being given over to death, He was led away and a rope put about His neck or His loins: *"He was led as a sheep to the slaughter." (Isaiah 53:7)*.

The direction in which Jesus Christ was led was outside the city. He was not to die in Jerusalem. Multitudes of prophets had died in Jerusalem. The temple was the central place of sacrifice. However, He was not to be offered there. He was an offering of another kind. He was not lying upon their altars. He was to die outside the city. The Jews treated Him as a flagrant offender who must be executed at the Tyburn of the city in the appointed place of doom known as Calvary or Golgotha.

Jesus Christ had to die outside Jerusalem because He was not dying for Jerusalem nor was He dying for Israel alone. The effect of His atonement was not circumscribed by the walls of a city or by the bounds of a race. In Him, all the nations of the earth were to be blessed. So, out in the open, He had to die to show that He was to reconcile both Jews and Gentiles unto God.

"And He that same Jesus Himself] is the propitiation (the atoning sacrifice) for our sins, and not for ours alone but also for [the sins of] the whole world "(1 John 2:2).

Jesus Christ marked the road with crimson drops. Jesus Christ was not borne or carried together with His Bride. He walked carrying His cross.

Mankind easily finds so much applause for earthly Princes. But they found none for the King of kings.

Jesus Christ, the darling of the church, lonely, continued with the wedding procession along the way in His great sorrow. He traversed the rugged path of suffering. He went along the path with a heavy heart and heavy footsteps. He remained calm in the face of His enemies. He did not say a word against His Bride, the Church. When Zipporah saw her child bleeding, she said to Moses her husband: *"Surely a bloody husband art thou to me"*. (Exodus 4:25). Jesus Christ endured unending anguish, yet He did not say to His Bride: *"You are a costly bride to me for causing me to experience all of this shame and bloodshed"*. But He generously offered His life; He poured out His own heart, and He did not criticize.

Jesus Christ suffered the cross while despising the shame because He had budgeted for the greatest expense. Through it all, the faithful bridegroom paved a royal road of mercy for His bride.

Just as Prince Charles and Princess Diana, after the nuptials, rode in a 1902 State Landau carriage, the Church, the Bride and Jesus Christ, her Bridegroom, rode through the world in such a glorious carriage. But this is the age of concealment—the mystical Solomon and His beloved Solyma are both present on Earth, but they are unseen by men. The day is coming when both Jesus Christ and His Bride shall be revealed in glory before the eyes of all men.

"Little did Jesus Christ's abuser know that the crucifixion was a wedding procession for Him and His Bride."

Jesus Christ Was Affected By Notable Effects Of Suffering

Jesus Christ, the Son of God, became an ambassador in a chain. A King in chains — the God-Man sent, bound to take His trial in the Court of the high Priest, Caiaphas. Jesus' enemies chained Him because of their cowardice. They were terrified of Him, and conscience had turned them all into cowards, so it took all the care of a coward to keep Him in their grasp. He had no intention to attack them or even defend Himself. He had no desire to escape from their hands. Yet, they chained Him, probably fearing that He would break loose from them or, in some way, outwit them.

Strangely, those who arrested Him should never have been, thus, afraid of Jesus Christ who came alone from heaven, neither bearing arms nor wearing armor. He did not come to injure anyone. Jesus did not even defend or protect Himself against the hurts that His abusers inflicted upon Him. He did not defend Himself against Herod as a Babe in a manger. And all His life, Jesus exhibited manhood's weakness more than its strength. Yet, His enemies were often afraid of Him.

No doubt, there is a latent, a secret conviction in the minds of every sinner. They know that their victims are greater than they are. Even when cruel people hurt their victims with their infidel weapons, the former never seem to be satisfied with their own arguments. They continually seek fresh ways to hold victim's captive. Throughout their lives, the cruel people are afraid of their victims. They usually rant at their victims in a manner that is reminiscent of the boy who whistles as he races through the cemetery to maintain his courage.

Shame

Jesus Christ's enemies chained Him; no doubt, to increase the shame of His condition. He asked those who came to arrest Him in the Garden a multi-billion dollar question:

"At that time Jesus said to the crowds, "Have you come out with swords and clubs, as if I were a criminal, to capture me? Every day I used to sit, teaching in the temple, and you didn't arrest me. But all this has happened so that the writings of the prophets would be fulfilled. Then all the disciples deserted him and ran away." (Matthew 26:55 CBS).

The enemies bound Jesus Christ fast as though He was a criminal or a thief. Perhaps they tied His hands with tight cords behind His back to show that they regarded Him as a felon. The enemies of Jesus meant to portray that they were not taking Jesus Christ into a civil court where some cases of the law might be pending. Instead, they already condemned Him by the very act of binding Him. Jesus' enemies treated Him as if He were already sentenced to death. They treated Him as a criminal not worthy to stand a free man and plead for Himself before the judgment seat.

The Pain

Jesus Christ's enemies chained Him to increase His pain. He experienced a lot of discomfort and pain at the hands of His enemies:

"Then the company of soldiers, the commander, and the Jewish officials arrested Jesus and tied him up" (John 18:12 CBS).

Jesus Christ's dolorous pain fell upon His Spirit. His spiritual suffering was altogether within the veil. No one could descry or describe it. He stood to strengthen, not to fight. He must fight alone. So, after applying some holy, cordial, or sacred anointing to the oppressed Champion who was on the verge of fainting, He, our great Deliverer, received strength from His Father and rose to the last of His battles. They drew a picture of Him; they carved a piece of wood or ivory, but they did not know His soul's suffering. They could not enter into them. The same people who had previously cried, *"Hosanna!"* chanted with a loud voice *"Crucify Him! Crucify Him!"*

THE LACK

It was fitting that every word of our Lord on the cross be collected and preserved. Not a bone of Him shall be broken, so no word of His on the cross shall be lost. Each utterance contains a wealth of meaning that no man can fully express, and when combined, they form a vast ocean of thought that no human line can comprehend.

Jesus Christ, after He had endured so much scourging and so many torturing, was crucified. And whiles on the cross, He cried out: *"I thirst"* (John 19:28). His cry was the complaint of a man. He demonstrated His humanity by going through the pains of manhood. Angels are not thirsty. As some have called Him, a phantom could not suffer in His fashion. But Jesus Christ truly suffered, not only from the more refined pangs of delicate and sensitive minds, but also from the rougher and more common pangs of flesh and blood. Thirst is a commonplace misery, such as may happen to peasants or beggars. It's a real pain, not a fantasy or a dreamland nightmare. Thirst is an evil of universal manhood, not a royal grief. Jesus Christ is the brother to the afflicted and most humble of our race.

He is the Maker of the ocean and the waters that are above the firmament. The hand of Jesus Christ stays or opens the bottles of heaven. He sends rain upon the evil and upon the good. *"The sea is His, and He made it"* (Psalm 95:5). All fountains and springs are of His digging. Jesus Christ pours out the streams that run among the hills; the torrents that rush down the mountains and the flowing rivers that enrich the plains. One would have said: *If Jesus Christ were thirsty, He would not tell anyone*. After all, the clouds and rains would be glad to refresh His brow. The brooks and streams would have joyously flowed at Jesus Christ's feet. Despite the fact that He was God of all and had fully taken on the form of a servant and was perfectly made in the likeness of sinful flesh, Jesus Christ cried out in a fainting voice: *"I thirst."* (John 19:28).

THE DEATH

We hold the last words of decent men in high regard. But who can tell how much their final thought is worth? The disciples' most honorable responsibility was gathering and preserving every word spoken by Jesus Christ while He was hanging on the cross. If His bone was not broken, His word was not forgotten either.

There are seven of Jesus Christ's last words that have been recorded. Seven represents completion and perfection; it is the sum of the three members of the Triune Godhead. Jesus Christ was the embodiment of His Father, Himself, and the Holy Spirit. The three are summed up as being a Trinity in unity. And the Godhead ruled over all the four structures that make up the whole of creation:

the angel's world (Genesis 1:1, Job 38:4-11); the Human's world (Genesis 2:1&2:4); the kingdom's world (Isaiah 65:17-25); the new Heaven and the New Earth (Revelation 21:1).

Jesus Christ was perfect in every way, even His cries of despair. The one who is God became Man. He lived a life of perfect virtue and of total self-denial. He was all that life-long despised and rejected by men. He was a man of sorrows and acquainted with grief. His enemies were legion; His friends were few, and those few were faithless. He was, at last, delivered over into the hands of them that hated Him. He was arrested while in the act of prayer. He was arraigned before both the spiritual and temporal courts. He was robed in mockery and then unrobed in shame. He was mocked on a throne and then cruelly tied to a pillar. He was declared innocent. However, He was delivered up by the judge who ought to have preserved Him from His enemies. He was dragged through the streets of the same Jerusalem which had killed the prophets. The street crimsoned itself with the blood of the prophets' Master. He was brought to the cross. He was nailed fast to the cruel wood. The sun burned Him. His cruel wounds increased the fever. God forsook Him. His pitiful cry *"My God, my God, why hast thou forsaken me?"* contains the world's concentrated anguish.

In the final hour, pains and groans usually disintegrate the mind, making it impossible for the dying person to gather their thoughts. Even if a person who is dying is able to gather their thoughts, they are typically unable to express them in a way that other people can understand. In contrast, Jesus Christ displayed an exceptional mental clarity, strength, and agility during His final moments of life. No man will be able to adequately express the meaning that each of Jesus Christ's final words contained. And when they are all put together, they form a vast collection of thought beyond humankind's understanding. Even on the cross as everywhere else, we say of Jesus Christ:

"Never has a man talked as this Man talks." (John 7:46).

The summary of all of His last words on the cross proved that even amid all the anguish of His Spirit, Jesus Christ remained fully self-possessed. He was true to His forgiving nature. He was true to His kingly office and his filial relationship. He was true to His God and His love of the written word. He was true to His glorious work, and true to His faith in His Father. While hanging on the cross in a mortal combat with sin and Satan, Jesus Christ's heart was broken and His limbs were dislocated. It appeared heaven had failed Him, for the sun was veiled in darkness. Earth forsook Him, for *"His disciples forsook Him and fled."* (Matthew 26:56 KJV). He looked everywhere, and there was none to help Him. He cast His eyes around, and there was no man that could share His toil. He treaded the winepress alone, and of the people, there was none with Him. On and on, Jesus Christ went, determined to drink the last dreg of that cup that must not pass from Him if His Father's will was to be fulfilled.

At last, Jesus Christ cried: *"It is finished."* and He gave up the ghost. Someone out there may ask: What did Jesus Christ mean by *"It is finished?"* Perhaps, He meant that all types, promises, and prophecies had been fulfilled in Him at that point. He might also imply that the traditional Jewish sacrifices had been eliminated and their purpose had been defined. They had been completed—finished in Him. He may again mean that by death, He had fully fulfilled His willful obligation to obey God.

Further, Jesus Christ may also be emphasizing that the satisfaction He provided for God's justice was complete. The debt had now been completely erased down to the last penny. One offering offered in Jesus Christ's body on the cross served as the atonement and propitiation once and for all. For a very long time, Satan held a cup for humanity, and the content was hell. Jesus Christ drank everything in the cup. He did not take a sip, a pause, or a draught, and then stop. No! Jesus Christ drained the cup completely leaving nothing for any of His followers to drink. And Jesus Christ said: *"It is finished."* There was no better way to put it than what He did. He completely destroyed the power of Satan, sin, and death.

Jesus Christ, the Victor, joined the ranks to engage in combat with all of humanity's enmity: base and wicked thoughts, sexual immorality, stealing, murder, adultery, coveting, dangerous and destructive wickedness, deceit, evil deed, slander, evil speaking, malicious misrepresentation, abusiveness, pride, an uplifted heart against God and man, foolishness, etc. for the salvation of our souls.

Sin is the collective name for all humanity's enemy. And Jesus Christ confronted each of them and defeated them. He was nailed on the cross by dreadful and almost omnipotent sin. He, however, also nailed sin on the cross in that act. Both of them: Sin and Sin's destroyer did hang there together. In Jesus Christ, sin destroyed mankind, and through that destruction, Jesus Christ also destroyed sin.

At Golgotha, on the day of Jesus Christ's crucifixion, if one had passed beyond the gate of His speech, one would have desired to see the secret things which were transacted in the silent chambers of His souls in the moment of His departure. One would then have greatly valued the revelation. Apparently, there were revelations in Jesus Christ's thoughts that His tongue could not say to His disciples. Therefore, He said:

"But when He, the Spirit of Truth (the Truth-giving Spirit) comes, He will guide you into all the Truth (the whole, full Truth). For He will not speak His own message [on His own authority]; but He will tell whatever He hears [from the Father; He will give the message that has been given to Him], and He will announce and declare to you the things that are to come [that will happen in the future]" (John 16:13).

"For a very long time, Satan held a cup for humanity, and the content was hell. Jesus Christ drank everything in the cup. He did not take a sip, a pause, or a draught, and then stop. No! Jesus Christ drained the cup completely leaving nothing for any of His followers to drink."

CHAPTER 04

JESUS CHRIST'S HUMILIATION

I have come to understand that the life of Jesus Christ is the simplest lesson the bible has to teach. However, it is often the most difficult lesson for the Christian to learn. That simple lesson is that we must not look to ourselves for any solution in this life. Instead, we must look to Jesus Christ for all solutions. I admit how apt I have been to forget that which is the very Alpha of the gospel, its rudiments.

I offer, then, to you this very comforting reflection. In Jesus Christ's sufferings, I have everything akin to all my suffering. And you are also quite certain to find something akin to your own. In Jesus Christ's heart, you are quite sure to find a deep well of divine sympathy. It is very comforting to know that Jesus Christ can sympathize with us in all our afflictions. Jesus Christ can sympathize with you because He has suffered all kinds of suffering. And I may also add, for your comfort, that all Jesus Christ's suffering as you do, and His suffering with you must tend to shield you in your suffering.

I hear a plaintive voice over yonder say to me:

"I know that Annas, Caiaphas, Pilate, and Herod abused Jesus physically, emotionally, mentally, and psychologically. But I never read that He was sexually harassed, molested, or abused by anyone. How

can I hope He will suffer with the young girl or man who has been sexually molested and abused? How can such a sexually abused person trust Him?"

Dear friends, Jesus Christ was truly a Man. He was truly God, but He took up our nature. It is not in phantasm nor in fiction was Jesus Christ a man. But in reality, and in truth, He became one of us. He was born of a woman, wrapped in swaddling bands, fed from the breast. He grew as a child, obeyed His parents, and grew in stature and wisdom. He worked, walked, and grew tired as a man. He ate like us, fasted, and hungered.

Jesus Christ's Human nature was sustained, as ours is, by supplying it with food. Though on one occasion, He was sustained by divine power and fasted forty days and forty nights, yet as man, He ordinarily needed food. He drank and gave thanks both for food and drink. He slept with His head upon a pillow and rested upon the curb of the well of Sychar. He suffered all the innocent infirmities of our nature. He was a hungered Man, and was disappointed when, early in the morning, He came to a fig-tree seeking fruit, but found none. He was weary:

"Jesus, being wearied with His journey, sat thus on the well." (John 4:6 KJV).

After Jesus Christ's resurrection, He ate a piece of a broiled fish and a honeycomb to show that His body was real. In all things, Jesus Christ was made like unto His brethren. *"Himself took our infirmities and bare our sicknesses." (Matt 8:17 KJV).* He had human friendships. Friendship is natural to man. Scarcely is a person a human being who never had a friend to love. Men, in going through the world, make many acquaintances. But out of those are few special objects of esteem we call friends. All wise and good people have about them choice spirits with whom their intercourse is freer. In those people, their trust is more confident than in all others.

Jesus Christ still found it difficult to live here among us. Although He conducted Himself in a most patronizing manner, He must have been deeply disturbed and grieved by what He endured in this world of sinners. They were unsuitable companions for Him because of their drastically different worldviews from His and because they shared no traits in common with Him.

Jesus Christ was tempted in all ways. He was tempted by the Herodians and Sadducees, the openly skeptical, and the Pharisees and the Scribes, the professed religious. However cruel our abusers may be, they are not so numerous or fierce as Jesus Christ's. Yet, He did not sin. His humanity was our humanity to the full, but He was without sin. Sin is not essential to humanity: it is a disease of nature. Sin is not a feature found in humanity as it came from the Creator's hand. The man of men, in whom all true humanity is found in perfection, is Jesus Christ.

When He was condemned to be crucified, Jesus Christ's abuser forged the cruelest of falsehoods until their reproaches broke His heart. Moreover, it is a wonderful fact one could scarcely have imagined — but the record is clear: His executioners sexually abused Jesus during His crucifixion.

The idea that Jesus Christ was a victim of sexual abuse is almost always initially met with surprise and incredulity. Many people say that when they first heard the idea, it seemed absurd, even outrageous, or offensive. Some have gone as far as to suggest that it might be blasphemous and should not even be said. Yet, after hearing more about the gospel accounts and reflecting on those, people often change their minds. The idea of Jesus as a victim of sexual abuse no longer appears strange. What seems strange is that something so clear in the biblical text could be hidden for so long.

It is strange that Jesus Christ's sexual abuse could stay hidden in what amounts to plain sight within such well-known passages. Identifying the relevance of the sexual abuse of Jesus Christ during torture for consideration of sexual abuse is not to equate the two as the same. It does not mean that the two are interchangeable or viewed as identical. Sexual abuse takes different forms, and each form should be understood in its own terms and specificity. Even within a broad sub-category, such as childhood sexual abuse, the experience of victims varies dramatically.

CRUCIFIXION, THE CROWNING OF SIN

Crucifixion was used in the Roman world for more than just killing the victim. Crucifixions were designed to degrade and dehumanize the victim in the eyes of society at large. Most references to crucifixions are for the execution of men though there is evidence that women were also crucified (Josephus, Antiquities 18.3). The public display of crucifixion with a naked victim was a form of sexual humiliation for both male and female victims. This humiliation also warned the public about the terrible consequences of rebelling against those in power. The passion narratives offer details about the crucifixion of Jesus in which the sexual element is clear. According to Matthew (27:26–27), after being condemned by Pilate, Jesus was taken by the guards into the governor's headquarters (praetorium). In front of "the whole cohort" which likely numbered four hundred to five hundred soldiers, the guards *"stripped Jesus Christ and put a scarlet robe on him"* (Matthew 27:28 KJV).

Jesus Christ was mocked, beaten, and spat upon by a crowd of soldiers before being stripped again:

"And when they finished making sport of Him, they stripped Him of the robe and put Him own garments on Him and led Him away to be crucified (Matthew 27:31).

Clearly, the foregoing passage and its parallel in Mark 15:16–20 show that Jesus was first stripped naked to be mocked. The soldiers then stripped Him again and dressed Him for His journey through the city. They stripped Him the third time at the cross and exhibited Him naked on the cross until He died before the mocking crowd.

If Jesus Christ was also initially stripped to be flogged (Matthew 27:26), it brings the recorded stripping in Matthew to a total of four in the space of just six verses (Matthew 27:26–31). Each of Jesus Christ's stripping involved complete nakedness. John records in the following words:

"Then the soldiers, when they had crucified Jesus, took His garments and made four parts, one share for each soldier, and also the tunic (the long shirtlike undergarment). But the tunic was seamless, woven [in one piece] from the top throughout." (John 19:23).

Although the gospels do not specify that Jesus Christ died fully naked, the evidence favors a complete despoliation during the crucifixion. The person of Jesus Christ was stripped although our painters, for obvious reasons, covered Him upon the cross; there, Jesus Christ hanged—the naked Savior of a naked race.

When Adam and Eve were naked in the Garden, Jesus Christ's Father made them skin coats. He took from them the fig leaves with which they sought to hide their nakedness. He gave them something wherewith they might wrap themselves from the cold.

But on the cross, Jesus Christ's abusers parted His garments among themselves. They cast lots for the clothing of Jesus Christ leaving Him alone to face the ruthless storm of ridicule. He did not have a covering to conceal His shame.

Certainly, John, who gave the greatest attention to the scene, was so specific about every item of clothing that one would have the impression that nothing was left. The normal Roman pattern was to crucify criminals naked. Nakedness during execution was a sign of humiliation, vulnerability, and absolute powerlessness for both the Romans and the Jews, as shame and dishonor were integral factors in the punishment.

In artistic depictions of the crucifixion, the element of Jesus Christ's mistreatment has been minimized, including a loincloth. Most images cover the shame and humiliation intended by forced nakedness. It is imperative to emphasize that sexual abuse, whether or not it is part of the torture, is frequently used to humiliate and punish the victim.

Jesus Indeed Resurrected

To Jesus' disciples, His death meant the loss of His personal presence. It was a great joy for that small family to have Jesus as their Father, Friend, Brother, and Teacher all the time. They were saddened to think that they would no longer be able to hear His gentle voice or see His lovely face. It provided the disciple's incalculable satisfaction to go to Jesus with all their questions, run to Him in every moment of trouble, and turn to Him in every hour of grief. Joyful and all smiling were those disciples to have such a God-Man always in their company as He conversed with them in love, guided them by His perfect example, invigorated them by His beautiful presence, satisfied all their desires, and protected them from all illnesses: Flu, Cancer, Leprosy, Epilepsy, Blindness, Haemorhage Diabetes, etc.,

While the men had found other matters to attend to, and their duty called them away from the tomb of Jesus, Mary remained, hoping to learn more about her Lord and, at the very least, to learn where He had been laid to rest:

"But Mary remained standing outside the tomb sobbing. As she wept, she stooped down [and looked] into the tomb." (John 20:11).

Mary, a loyal disciple of Jesus Christ, wept as if her heart would shatter. Where had her Lord disappeared? What had the cruel soldiers done to His precious dead body? She had seen her beloved's dead body wrapped in spices and beautiful linen and laid in Joseph's tomb; where was it now? But there she stood, the tomb clearly empty of anything but rituals; where was the body? What new humiliations had the cruel ones heaped on it? What cruel abuse had that dear, disfigured body now been subjected to? Mary stood there, overcome with emotion, weeping as only Love can weep when her beloved thing is in trouble.

When Mary looked down, she saw two angels sitting, one at the head and the other at the feet where Jesus' corpse had laid. When the angels asked Mary: *"Woman, why do you weep?"* (John 20:13a), She replied to them directly:

"Because they have taken away my Lord, and I know not where they have laid him." (John 20:13 KJV).

As if in a dream:

"On saying this, she turned around and saw Jesus standing [there], but she did not know (recognize) that it was Jesus." (John 20:14).

While Mary stood looking into the tomb, Jesus was behind her, and though she was unaware of it, His presence had an effect on her. She had been speaking to the angels and answering their questions when she became aware of someone standing just behind her. Nobody could have imagined that Mary Magdalene would ever forget the melody of her beloved's voice, but she did. She was so far away from knowing her Lord that she mistook Him for an enemy rather than a friend. She envisioned the gardener carrying the body of Jesus away. Mary assumed he was so afraid of having a corpse in the vicinity of his gardening that he had hidden it in a spot where no one could see it. So, she endeared herself before him and volunteered to carry away the design to which she had anticipated he would protest:

"…Sir, if you carried Him away from here, tell me where you have put Him and I will take Him away." (John 20:15d).

He, to whom Mary talked, had not taken her beloved; rather, He had delivered Him to her; indeed, He was the beloved! When Jesus said to her:

"Mary!" (John 16:1a) She recognized Him and exclaimed: "Rabboni!" (John 16:1b). One word of love from Jesus' lips: "Mary!" elicited another word of reverence from her lips: "Rabboni!" "Rabboni" is a Hebrew word that means "Master", "My Master" or "Great Master".

Jesus had greeted Mary by name, and she inherited that all-powerful voice. He was her Master because He had the miraculous ability to know and move her heart. There stood Jesus Christ, and Mary recognized Him, and the first reaction of her being was to touch and hold Him, lest He would disappear.

However, Jesus the Master prevented her from getting too close, saying:

"…Touch me not; for I am not yet ascended to my Father." (John 17:1KJV).

Mary, unlike Thomas, did not need to place her finger in the print of Jesus' nails or press her hand into His side to know He was the One. She did not need it since she knew He was Jesus Christ and that He had resurrected from the dead. Thomas doubted that Jesus had resurrected, and the other disciples had some unanswered questions. Therefore, Jesus decided to give them some signs that Mary did not require.

"Eight days later His disciples were again in the house, and Thomas was with them. Jesus came, though they were behind closed doors, and stood among them and said, Peace to you! Then He said to Thomas, Reach out your finger here, and see My hands; and put out your hand and place [it] in My side. Do not be faithless and incredulous, but [stop your unbelief and] believe!" (John 20:26-27).

*"Men, in going through the world,
make many acquaintances. But
out of those are few special
objects of esteem we call friends."*

CHAPTER 05

CONTRACTION FOR THE BIRTH OF THE HOLY SPIRIT

Jesus Christ, after being resurrected, would not ascend to heaven until He had established the fact of His resurrection on a firm foundation that could never be broken. Thus, He remained on earth for forty days after His resurrection before ascending to the Father in heaven because it had to take forty days to establish His identity and show evidence that He had indeed risen.

In the Bible, forty days is a significant period in Jesus' ministry. He had been in the desert for forty days, tempted by the devil; so, it seemed fitting for Him to stay here for forty days of victory on the premises of His first major war and victory. His appearance was not a solitary vision seen by one or two believers. He was clearly shown to a large crowd as their Lord and Master who had been brutally crucified yet had risen from the grave. They were sufficient to demonstrate to the world that Jesus had definitely risen from the dead, not as a ghost, but in true flesh and blood.

Throughout those forty days, Jesus appeared in so many places to so many witnesses and His disciples in so many different ways to demonstrate how real His resurrection was. The proof for Jesus' resurrection became profuse and convincing.

Magdalene and James saw Jesus alone while the eleven saw Him among them. He spoke with the two on the trip to Emmaus. Five hundred believers saw the resurrected Jesus all at once. He provided infallible proof that He had truly risen from the dead, which has remained with us today as a historical fact (1 Corinthians 15:6). Thus, it is impossible for five hundred believers to be misled all at once to think that they had seen the resurrected Jesus. And, even if they might be misled, it is unlikely that two or three people in separate locations who had had the most intimate encounter with the resurrected Jesus Christ could have been misled.

Skepticism led Thomas to place his finger in the mark of Jesus' nails and drive his hand into His side to ensure that He was the Lord he had served. Nothing could be more convincing than Thomas', the skeptical inspector's assessment.

"Jesus said to him, Because you have seen Me, Thomas, do you now believe (trust, have faith)? Blessed and happy and to be envied are those who have never seen Me and yet have believed and adhered to and trusted and relied on Me." (John 20:29).

However, it was critical to the greatest degree that the fact of Jesus' resurrection be proven beyond all doubt, and it is now the best-established truth in all history. The forty days Jesus Christ spent on earth were sufficient to establish to future generations that He indeed rose from the dead. During those forty days, Jesus not only established the profound truth about His resurrection, but He also consoled His disciples. He wiped away the tears shed by the disciples during His crucifixion and helped them understand that they no longer needed to mourn His death.

Those forty days were extraordinary days, so different from Jesus' previous life on earth. No Scribes or Pharisees opposed Him throughout the forty days following His resurrection, and no spiteful Jews took up stones to stone Him. Nobody bothered or interrupted Jesus Christ. Those were the golden days when the doves of peace rested on the motionless waters, and not a wave disturbed the peace. Each of Jesus' disciples rejoiced to think that their crucified Lord and Master was suddenly among them, not only alive, but also surrounded by a supernatural safety and radiance that no one could disrupt.

Jesus' enemies who desired His death on earth were as silent as the dead corpses. None of them possessed a spiritual eye or ear to view or hear Him during His afterlife on earth. So, Jesus had all the time in the world to clear His disciples' minds of any remaining doubts about everything He had taught them.

Even though Thomas has been singled out as a doubter, none of Jesus' disciples were without some doubt. Peter and the others' going back to fishing was a sure indication of doubt.

"Simon Peter said to them, I am going fishing! They said to him, And we are coming with you! So they went out and got into the boat, and throughout that night they caught nothing." (John 21:3).

As a result, the resurrected Jesus had to address several of His disciples individually since they had particular needs. He had to encourage Magdalene's heart, overcome Thomas' doubt, and caution and motivate Peter, the uncontested leader of the apostles. So, Jesus had to act and speak in such a way that each of them was completely convinced of His identity and the nature of His resurrected body. Therefore, He addressed them:

"See My hands and My feet, that it is I myself! Feel and handle Me and see, for a spirit does not have flesh and bones, as you see that I have."(Luke 24:39).

The great Commander-In-Chief could not return to His Father until He had attended to every mentally and emotionally wounded soldier and put the entire army in order, and prepared them for their future assignments. So, before His final departure, the resurrected Jesus issued His final orders, marshaled His troops, and placed them in their ranks. Jesus gave commissions to His present and future disciples, saying:

"Go then and make disciples of all the nations, baptizing them into the name of the Father and of the Son and of the Holy Spirit..." (Matthew 28:19).

And to Peter, Jesus directly told three times: *"Feed my lambs."* (John 21:15), *"Tend My sheep."* (John 21:16), and *"Feed My sheep."* (John 21:17).

Thus, Jesus gave His disciples directions as to how to act. He organized them as an army unit, ordered their line of battle, gave them His commands, and braced them all for their coming struggle. He also gave them His commands, prepared them, and bade them to march to battle and victory.

Jesus told every one of His disciples to stay in Jerusalem until they were endowed with power from on high; all Christians have the same direct mandate for all eternity. All Jesus did was to follow His resurrection and prepare the disciples for the safe delivery of the Holy Spirit.

Before His death, Jesus told His disciples:

"I have still many things to say to you, but you are not able to bear them or to take them upon you or to grasp them now." (John 16:12).

So, by preparing them for delivery after He rose from the dead, the disciples were able to bear much more. And there is no question that the resurrected Jesus gave revelations to them at that time because the resurrected Jesus possessed even more resurrection infinite wisdom. And all of Jesus' resurrection words brought contraction into their wombs.

According to Luke, Jesus opened their minds to receive the Scripture and opened the Scripture so that their minds might grasp them (Luke 24:45).

Jesus also prepared the disciples for the longer-lasting pain of His departure: He so exalted their minds and spirits that we never hear of their bemoaning His ascension. He convinced them that it was better for Him to leave so that the Comforter could come to them. He also consorted with them, bestowed His Spirit on them, and filled them with His peace:

"And having said this, He breathed on them and said to them, Receive the Holy Spirit!" (John 20:22).

All of the words that came from the resurrected Jesus prepared the disciples to enter the prenatal delivery phase:

"And behold, I will send forth upon you what My Father has promised; but remain in the city [Jerusalem] until you are clothed with power from on high." (Luke 24:49).

And one hundred and twenty of them, all pregnant with the Holy Spirit, climbed across the grassy fields, moist with the frost, to the maternity ward in the Upper Room to wait until Jesus Christ would induce them to labor.

"But you shall receive power (ability, efficiency, and might) when the Holy Spirit has come upon you..." (Acts 1:8).

A Farewell Service Of Jesus Christ

Luke tells us where Jesus brought His disciples from and to for His accession:

Then He conducted them out as far as Bethany, and, lifting up His hands, He invoked a blessing on them." (Luke 24:50).

And in the Acts of the Apostles, he recounts the momentous event as taking place on "the mount called Olivet" which is a Sabbath day's trip from Jerusalem. Let us consider the scenario for a moment. There were eleven apostles assembled around Jesus Christ, and possibly some more, including the two with whom Jesus walked alongside on the road to Emmaus. They had traveled from Jerusalem to Bethany and Olivet. The Bible is silent on whether they walked through the streets early in the morning, late in the afternoon, or late in the evening. If that is the case, could the residents of the town actually see Jesus Christ? If they could see Jesus, how would they have looked at the Messiah whom they had seen nailed to the cross on Calvary, suddenly alive and walking through their streets? How many children and adults would have fled in fear believing they had seen a ghost?

Jesus and His disciples continued to cross the Kedron, the horrific river where the defilements of the temple were washed away. They then walked through Gethsemane following the serpentine way until they reached the summit of Olivet. From that vantage point, Jesus could see Jerusalem on one side and Bethany on the other side. Jesus could have been speaking with His disciples or, at the very least, answering all of Peter's last-minute questions during the time.

"He said to them, It is not for you to become acquainted with and know what time brings [the things and events of time and their definite periods] or fixed years and seasons (their critical niche in time), which the Father has appointed (fixed and reserved) by His own choice and authority and personal power." (Acts 1:7).

If the disciples had been members of the contemporary Church of Pentecost, they would have sung farewell songs and danced with Jesus. Then, one of the apostles would have read from a plaque engraved with Jesus' picture citations written by the presbytery. While the disciples were still enjoying Jesus' delightful company, Jesus lifted His pierced hands and proceeded to pour over them words of love, inspiration, affirmation, hope, unity, and peace:

Then He *conducted them out as far as Bethany, and, lifting up His hands, He invoked a blessing on them." (Luke 24:50).*

To their surprise, while they were receiving Jesus' blessing, He began to ascend from the earth above them all! The disciples must have been stunned and horrified as Jesus arose and went up leisurely and majestically like a groom walking down the aisle on His wedding day.

Imagine the disciples' staring at Him until He became less visible to their surprised stare. While the disciples were looking, Jesus ascended into semi and climbed quickly to the cloud realms. They were taken aback when a sparkling cloud resembling a heavenly chariot came and carried Jesus away:

"And when He had said this, even as they were looking [at Him], He was caught up, and a cloud received and carried Him away out of their sight." (Acts 1:9).

The cloud hid Jesus from human eyes and hovered between Jesus and the disciples exactly as the Holy Spirit had done in the beginning over the face of the waters.

"The Spirit of God was moving (hovering, brooding) over the face of the waters."(Genesis 1:2b).

The resurrected Jesus arose by His own power (Holy Spirit) and majesty; He did not require the help of humans or angels. And how delighted the angels would have been to return to earth as they had done at His birth in the wilderness, and at His grave - how eagerly they would have served Him! But, at least, in His journey from earth to heaven, Jesus did not require their service. He demonstrated His Deity's inherent authority by leaving the earth whenever He pleased defying the law of gravitation, and suspending the laws that normally control matter.

An Opened Heaven, A Blissful Home, And The "Way"

The disciples had known Jesus Christ in the flesh for three and a half years, but on their watch, each of them experienced the reality that they would no longer know Him in the flesh. They were naturally captivated by the spot of Jesus' accession: Still looking up, they remained there for a long time, heartbroken yet fascinated.

However, Jesus does not want any of His disciples to stay passive for an extended period of time because He is well aware of the endless ramifications. Apparently, the disciples may have stood there until their surprise turned to anxiety, worry, dread, and hopelessness. They had stayed long enough, and their extended stare and passivity needed to be interrupted. So, God dispatched two angels, as He had before, to meet Mary and the women at Jesus' empty tomb.

God's angels appeared in human form so as not to terrify them and in white robes as though to remind them that everything was bright and joyful. And those two white-robed angels stood close to the disciples as though they were eager to join their inner wordless discourse. The men in white robes initiated a conversation because none of the eleven bewildered disciples would break the silence. They addressed them in the normal angelic manner asking a question that had its own response, and then proceeded to tell them their message. The angels enquired in the same tone as they had previously spoken to the women.

"And as [the women] were frightened and were bowing their faces to the ground, the men said to them, Why do you look for the living among [those who are] dead?" (Luke 24:5).

In the same tone, as they had informed the women He was not there but had risen, they also told the disciples:

"Men of Galilee, why do you stand gazing into heaven? This same Jesus, Who was caught away and lifted up from among you into heaven will return in [just] the same way in which you saw Him go into heaven. (Acts 1:11).

The angels revealed their knowledge of the disciples by referring to them as "Men of Galilee". And by doing so, the angels reminded the disciples that the latter were still on earth, particularly Galilee their birthplace. When the apostles were awakened from their slumber by the impending delivery of the "Holy Spirit" and the "Gospel", they promptly mustered themselves for labor; they did not need to delay; then, hurriedly they went to Jerusalem to the maternity ward.

I implore every Christian to consider Jesus Christ's ascension in these simple but graceful aspects: an opened heaven, a blissful home, and the "Way" sanctified and paved by His wonderful feet. The heavens opened above us, and Jesus Christ passed through dispatching gifts to humanity.

"Therefore it is said, When He ascended on high, He led captivity captive [He led a train of vanquished foes] and He bestowed gifts on men." (Ephesians 4:8).

Furthermore, Bethany was just beneath the disciples' feet from the mountain where Mary, Martha, and Lazarus lived joyfully since Jesus visited them regularly. Thus, Jesus left us the church where He eternally lives as a family, for us to imitate and establish our own happy home where we live.

Then Jesus left us a path, often walked by His heavenly feet, and the disciples were to return to Jerusalem by that path — Jerusalem, from whence Jesus had brought them to His ascension. Even if they had forgotten due to amazement, the vision of angels after the accession brought them back to consciousness, and they obeyed the command.

"And behold, I will send forth upon you what My Father has promised; but remain in the city [Jerusalem] until you are clothed with power from on high." (Luke 24:49).

"An opened heaven, a blissful home, and the "Way""

CHAPTER 06

THE CONDUCT OF THE PARTURIENT DISCIPLES IN THE MATERNITY WARD

Because the way childbirth is handled can significantly impact both the delivery and the whole delivery experience, it is one of the most important aspects of maternity treatment. To boost the pregnant patient's confidence in themselves and those who serve her, the nurses' and caregivers' every word and action should be correct and thoroughly planned.

In the presence of parturient disciples in the maternity Upper Room, thoughtless conversation, silliness, and discussions about other patients had no place. Every effort was made to create the pleasant, happy, yet respectable environment that childbirth necessitates. Certain terminologies such as "Immorality", "impurity", "indecency", "Idolatry", "sorcery", "enmity", "strife", "jealousy", "anger", "ill temper", "selfishness", "divisions", "dissensions", "party spirit" (factions, sects with peculiar opinions, heresies), "envy", "drunkenness", "carousing", etc. associated with fleshly practices induce stress and anxiety in the patient (Disciple) and prevent smooth labor.

While our human nature makes it impossible to resist most of those behaviors, Jesus has provided preferable non-harmful alternatives. Thus, the disciples in the maternity room used terminologies such as "love", "joy", "peace", "patience", "kindness", "goodness" (benevolence), "faithfulness", "gentleness" and "self-control". Everything that happened at the infirmary in Jerusalem when the disciples' labor began became more familiar and less frightening because the resurrected Jesus Christ, through words, depicted imaginary labor to the patients (Disciples) prior to real parturition. Jesus instructed them that the patients (Disciples) should be placed in a room or area that would allow them appropriate privacy when praying.

If a patient (Disciple) has to share space with others, privacy should be prioritized during examinations and treatments (Prayer, Worship, and Listening to Sermons). Because hospital facilities (Church, Upper Room) vary considerably, the accommodations provided to the admitted patient (Disciple) will vary greatly.

Every gynecologist (Jesus) should be able to devote their full attention to the patient (Disciple) without prejudice or heightened tensions caused by the existence of fleshy practices. To ensure uninterrupted delivery, every work of the flesh must be kept out of the Holy Spirit's maternity room just as other relatives should be kept out of the secular delivery room.

Thus, one hundred and twenty people gathered from different directions, and their steps intersected on Mount Zion's Upper Room. Those men and women were not like the majority of Christians in the twentieth century. They would not try to rationalize their disobedience of God's commands. Jesus had shown them true love in various forms and said:

"If you keep My commandments [if you continue to obey My instructions], you will abide in My love and live on in it, just as I have obeyed My Father's commandments and live on in His love." (John 15:10).

Jesus Christ further said:

"But you shall receive power (ability, efficiency, and might) when the Holy Spirit has come upon you, and you shall be My witnesses in Jerusalem and all Judea and Samaria and to the ends (the very bounds) of the earth. (Acts 1:8).

Such Believers grasped the full meaning of their salvation, and they fully obeyed Christ's instruction which enabled them to effectively do the ministry work. Obeying Jesus Christ became a natural thing to the disciples because of their total obedience. Their devotion to Jesus Christ was real.

The disciples realized the need to tarry for unction after having been instructed by Jesus to wait for the endowment of power. They also realized the importance to strictly have confidence and belief in His promises. They never questioned Him because all the many things Jesus spoke about Himself when He was with them had come to pass: His many trials, His rejection, His death, His burial, His resurrection, and many other things. Because of the fulfillment of those prophecies, His disciples trusted Jesus' words in the same way that a pregnant woman trusts, without a doubt, that no matter how long her pregnancy lasts, she will give birth to a baby. So, as a day grew into a week, the disciples waited.

The Disciples' Prolonged Labor

Jesus Christ preached to multitudes of people for three and a half years. And one hundred and twenty of them became heavily pregnant with the "Gospel" and the "Church". As their due date approached, Jesus Christ, the great Physician, directed that they remain in Jerusalem, at the hospital where the maternity ward was located until they were blessed with power from on high to deliver.

The word "Prolonged labor" indicates "time" as the primary deciding unit. While hours of labor are significant, they are not the only aspect to consider. In our everyday lives, first-time mothers (Primipara) typically take 12 to 19 hours to deliver a baby, whereas mothers who have previously delivered children (Multipara) may take as little as 14 hours. Prolonged labor is usually determined during or after the delivery process based on whether the cervix is thinned and opened properly during labor. Many reasons can contribute to prolonged labor, including a large baby, an abnormal unborn baby position where a baby comes out any way other than head first, a small birth canal, weak contractions, etc. All of those factors are usually discovered after the fact.

It will remain this way throughout history; everything about the Godhead: the Father, the Son, and the Holy Spirit is a mystery. And it goes without saying that all mysterious beings and things are not pleasant to the godless. The Roman soldiers clearly demonstrated this; they would not have trembled and fallen as dead men when they beheld angels:

"And those keeping guard were so frightened at the sight of him that they were agitated and they trembled and became like dead men." (Matthew 28:4).

It is also true that, whether we acknowledge it or not, even the godly, in their best condition, are often out of sync with everything that is beneficial for us.

Jesus Christ had given His disciples the spiritual perception of the Holy Spirit. However, they did not have a complete understanding and experience of Him until He appeared. Throughout His earthly ministry, Jesus Christ put His people to the test in a variety of ways so that He could select only those fit for the possession of the world. On one occasion, He asked the whole disciples:

"...Will you also go away? [And do you too desire to leave Me?]"(John 6:67).

Jesus encountered multitudes of people both before and after His resurrection. After His resurrection, He appeared to 500 people on one occasion. But Luke only accounts for 120 people gathered in an upper room, so where were the other 380 people? They were undoubtedly impacted, and it is reasonable to suppose that Jesus revealed Himself to them because they were believers. But something happened between their encounter with the resurrected Jesus Christ and their encounter with the Holy Spirit.

Jesus Christ was much too clever to be concerned with the number of disciples or converts He had. He was more concerned with quality than quantity. He delighted over one sinner who repented, but millions of sinners who only pretended to repent would have brought Him no joy. Jesus' heart yearns for the authentic and despises the counterfeit. He craves for substance, yet the shadow can never appease Him. In order to live a living church like good grain in the soil, free of any contamination, and in the specific instance of the coming of the Third Person of the Godhead, there was a justifiable need for a "Prolonged labor."

It is safe to say that throughout the ten days that the disciples prayed, sang, and worshiped God, Jesus removed all anomalies that could prevent their safe and smooth delivery of the "Gospel" and the "Church". By the end of the tenth day, grace had prepared 120 wombs from the many wombs suitable for Jesus' use so that the Church would be born through them. So, based on the singularity of the Holy Spirit's birth, I will replace the word "Prolonged labor" with the broader term "Remarkable labor".

Attitude Of The Disciples In The Labor Ward

The disciples' anticipation caused them to climb the stairs that hope had created, and bowing on their knees with one accord in prayer, they all looked through the window that Jesus' love had opened:

"All of these with their minds in full agreement devoted themselves steadfastly to prayer, [waiting together] with the women and Mary the mother of Jesus, and with His brothers." (Acts 1:14)

It suited God to make prayer an abundant and joyful stream through which all our gracious graces flow. In prayer, the disciples, who were pregnant to give birth, acknowledged their Master with reverence and acknowledged Him to be the source of every good and perfect gift. Their eyes were lifted to the opened heavens while their knees were bent to the earth in the humility of admitted helplessness, and thus they waited.

All the spiritual people of Israel's twelve tribes waited for the first coming of Jesus Christ before He came into the world. They were certain that He would come, yet many of them died without seeing what they were hoping for:

"These people all died controlled and sustained by their faith, but not having received the tangible fulfillment of [God's] promises, only having seen it and greeted it from a great distance by faith, and all the while acknowledging and confessing that they were strangers and temporary residents and exiles upon the earth" (Hebrews 11:13).

Simeon and Anna were among those waiters ("waiting for the consolation of Israel.") who were found in the temple when Mary brought the Baby Jesus.

They had turned grey while waiting, but they were still there: "them that looked for redemption in Jerusalem"

Finally, Simeon could say:

"And now, Lord, You are releasing Your servant to depart (leave this world) in peace, according to Your word." (Luke 2:29).

The words "walk" and "wait" characterize practically the entirety of the Christian experience. When properly understood, waiting is both active and passive, vibrant and patient, and waiting on the Lord requires as much spiritual courage as a soldier who fights off their opponents. So, the disciples were to go to Jerusalem and wait. Jesus did not tell them how long they would have to wait; He simply told them to wait, and they did exactly that. The disciples were willing to wait because they believed the promise would come true. However, how they spent the ten days waiting was vital to the safe and successful labor.

Their Prospect

The disciple's prospect was that on the set time, the promised Holy Spirit would come and endue them with power from on high. Whiles they waited in the maternity ward (Upper Room), all doubts were erased from their minds. They were not afraid that, after all, their supposed belief was not a true one, for Jesus had proved it by His ascension to heaven.

So, their eyes were looking toward the opened heavens, and somehow, they hoped, if not quite a persuasion, that He who was to come would come. And so, though the Holy Spirit tarried, they all, with accord in prayer, tarried for Him. The behavior of the disciples is equally applicable to every Christian when we come into some personal waiting period, even if not exactly of their kind. Whatever it is that we wait on God for, He will surely come.

It is applicable to every child of God who has been laboring for Jesus Christ in any district which seemed strikingly barren, where the stones of the field seemed to break the plowshare. Still believe on, beloved; for very often, the most unfruitful soil will perhaps repay the Christian after a while with a hundred-fold harvest.

The prospect may be uncertain, but wait; for the promise will come no matter what.

Their Posture

The disciples were in the Labor Ward like soldiers on guard waiting for the actual labor time. It was almost time for their delivery; how could they occupy themselves until their water would break and the Baby (Holy Spirit) would come? Well, they had to wait in the Labor Ward (Upper Room) with patience and endurance as long as God had appointed it.

Whatever contractions and labor pain were yet to come, whatever strong cramping in the abdomen, groin, as an aching feeling, they had to bear them all. A parturient woman does not leave the labor ward and go home because she feels pain or the baby is delayed. At the least, her life falls in the hands of the physicians, yet she remains at the hospital. Thus, the disciples in the Upper Room patiently waited.

Like the parturient woman, the disciples remained hopeful in watching for the hour at which the baby would begin to drop. They kept their eyes towards the opened heavens and looked for the first grey sign of the coming of the Promised Holy Spirit.

While the disciples patiently waited and watched, they maintained patient endurance and hopeful watching. They were in one accord; hence, they gave one another mutual encouragement. They were like travelers who had been shipwrecked and, thus, gave one another a hand and said:

"Brother, Sister, Mother, Father, very soon the Promise will come after all."

It is, thus, not for any Christian to say they have waited for too long, and so they are quitting. Let us look for every sign of the promise appearing and be ever listening for the sound of His chariot wheels. As we await God's promises, let every Christian take hold of one another's hand.

Their Petition

It would have been very unbecoming if the disciples had continued to pray aloud nonstop for ten days. There would have been no chance for Peter to preach and the rest to hear. There would have been a little possibility for friendly conversation, using the bathroom, or any other of life's necessities, while the noise of the many continuous voices would have convinced their neighbors that their God was not a considerate Father.

Because they all committed to devoting themselves to prayer and were unable to pray for 240 hours without ceasing, it is clear that they did not solely use audible words throughout their prayers. It was never Jesus' intention, and it never will be, for His disciples' mouths, tongues, throats, lungs, rips, hands, legs, etc., to be always active.

Viewed from all points, prayers are of many sorts. No two genuine prayers from different people can be precisely alike, let alone 120 people. Master artists do not often multiply the same painting. They prefer to give expression to fresh ideas as often as they grasp the pencil.

Prayers may be divided into several different forms and orders. A prayer may be public or private, vocal, mental, protracted, or ejaculatory.

There is a wordless prayer:

"The poor and needy are seeking water when there is none; their tongues are parched with thirst. I the Lord will answer them; I, the God of Israel, will not forsake them." (Isaiah 41:17).

There is also a heart prayer:

"Hannah was speaking in her heart; only her lips moved but her voice was not heard. So Eli thought she was drunk. Eli said to her, How long will you be intoxicated? Put wine away from you. But Hannah answered, No, my lord, I am a woman of a sorrowful spirit. I have drunk neither wine nor strong drink, but I was pouring out my soul before the Lord." (1 Samuel 1:13-15).

There is deprecatory prayer in which we deprecate the wrath of God and entreat Him to turn away His fierce anger, withdraw His rod, and sheath His sword. Deprecatory prayers are offered at all times when calamity is to be feared and when sin has provoked God to jealousy.

Then there are supplicatory prayers in which we supplicate blessings and implore mercies from the liberal hand of God and entreat the heavenly Father to supply our wants out of His riches in glory by Christ Jesus:

"And my God will liberally supply (fill to the full) your every need according to His riches in glory in Christ Jesus." (Philippians 4:19).

There are prayers that are personal in which the suppliant pleads mainly concerning themselves. And there are pleadings that are intercessory, in which, like Abraham, the petitioner intercedes for Sodom or entreats that Ishmael might live before God.

"And [he] said to God, Oh, that Ishmael might live before You" (Genesis 17:18)

Prayer may be salted with confession, perfumed with thanksgiving, sung to praises, or wept out with groaning. Prayer, no matter what form it takes, must originate from the heart. Prayer with the lips, bended knee, and an outstretched hand is meaningless if the heart is absent. When they bow their knee in what they believe is prayer to God, many Christians disrespect the God of heaven because, despite their numerous words, they only rebel against Him because their hearts do not match their words.

Prayer as a form and routine is only the skin; heart work is the meat. Words are the snail case, and heartfelt desire is the jewel.

As much as oxygen is in the earth's crust, many were the prayers of the one hundred and twenty disciples who convened in the Maternity Suit (Upper Room) of the Holy Spirit.

But without doubt, many of those prayers made the mercy seat become a place for the exhibition of spiritual selfishness. But on and after the day of Pentecost, the disciples learned to pray in the Language of the Holy Spirit. And the Master-Artist, the Holy Spirit, who is the Author of prayer, produced in each one of them and upon the tablets of each person's hearts different kinds of prayer. They received the spirit of brotherly kindness, unanimity, and love and a spirit of an earnest desire to bring down a blessing from God to all of humanity.

A Christian is someone who sees God's kingdom as manifested by the Holy Spirit's birth:

"Jesus answered, I assure you, most solemnly I tell you, unless a man is born of water and [even] the Spirit, he cannot not [ever] enter the kingdom of God." (John 3:5).

In that new birth, we learn to submit to Jesus Christ and find eternal life in Him. Faith in Jesus Christ washes away our sins on the cross and gives the sinner an inward life of righteousness. That faith admits the sinner to God's kingdom:

"But as many as did receive and welcome Him, He gave the authority (power, privilege, right to become the children of God, that is, to those who believe in (adhere to, trust in, and rely on) His name." (John 1:12).

God has made Jesus His Son the heir of all things, and created the worlds through Him. And He says of Him:

"Kiss the Son [pay homage to Him in purity], lest He be angry and you perish in the way, for soon shall His wrath be kindled. O blessed (happy, fortunate, and to be envied) are all those who seek refuge and put their trust in Him!" (Psalm 2:12).

It implies having power in prayer, communication with Jesus Christ, fellowship with the Holy Spirit, and bearing and producing all the pleasant and blessed fruits that are the fruits of rebirth. The Christian on earth becomes a member of both the spiritual and visible church while also enjoying the freedom and blessings that come with being God's child.

Thus, it behooves a Christian to be a member of the "Church of Christ", that body of faithful people called out by the Holy Spirit from among the rest of humanity and gathered to defend and spread the truth (Gospel).

A person who cannot see God's kingdom from the earth cannot see God's kingdom in heaven because they would be out of place in heaven. A person who has not been born again cannot enter heaven. There is an actual impossibility in their nature that precludes them from experiencing any heavenly delight.

Many people let their imaginations soar with open wings when they start talking about heaven. And all they can think about is the vision of the dwelling with its chrysolite, chrysoprasus, and jacinth foundations. They see dazzling gold streets, pearl gates, angels, seraphim, and cherubim.

On the other hand, they fail to consider the mood of heaven, the state established on earth, in the heart, by God's Spirit within the saints, which is the "Visa" to heaven.

As it is physically impossible for a camel to pass through a needle, so it is for a person who has not been regenerated to enjoy the joys of heaven.

"As it is physically impossible for a camel to pass through a needle, so it is for a person who has not been regenerated to enjoy the joys of heaven."

CHAPTER 07

THE MATERNITY WARD OF THE HOLY SPIRIT

For ten days, a total of one hundred and twenty disciples gathered in the maternity suite of Jerusalem's Upper Room, praying, singing, and blessing God as they awaited the birth of the Holy Spirit. They had been ordered by Jesus Christ, their Master, to remain in Jerusalem until they were endowed with strength from on high. Those men and women were not like the majority of Christians in the twentieth century. They would not try to rationalize their disobedience of God's commands. Jesus had shown them true love in various forms and had said to them: *"If you love Me, obey My commandments"* (John 14:15). He also emphasized that: *"…if a man loves Me, he will keep My words."* (John 14:24). Jesus Christ said:

"But you shall receive power (ability, efficiency, and might) when the Holy Spirit has come upon you, and you shall be My witnesses in Jerusalem and all Judea and Samaria and to the ends (the very bounds) of the earth. (Acts 1:8).

Those Christians understood their salvation, and their ability to work in the ministry Jesus had entrusted to them hinged on their obedience. They had taken every word of Jesus Christ to heart and were determined to comply or wither away in the effort. By walking along with Jesus Christ, the disciples learned His obedience until it became natural to them. Their commitment to Jesus Christ was not an act of deception. They did not believe they could disobey God's commands in thought, in word, and in action and still be justified in God's eyes without consequence.

Jesus Christ had instructed them to wait for power. They recognized their need for such an anointing. They did not expect to receive it by disregarding Jesus' command but by properly following it. All the disciples believed in Jesus' promises. They had no cause to question Him. They had every reason to believe in Him. Jesus had said many things, and they had all come true; every promise He had made during His three years of teaching had been fulfilled. He had told them that He would go through many trials; He would be rejected; He would die, be buried, and rise again on the third day. Every one of those things had happened.

And on the day of Pentecost, while the one hundred and twenty people waited in the maternity suit, Jesus honored His promise and sent forth the Holy Spirit.

"When suddenly there came a sound from heaven like the rushing of a violent tempest blast, and it filled the whole house in which they were sitting." (Acts 2:2).

God, thus, poured His Spirit from heaven upon mankind. The Spirit of God descended and now lives in the midst of the church. Christians now enter into Him and are baptized into the Holy Spirit while He enters into us and transforms our bodies into his temples.

"The Spirit of Truth, Whom the world cannot receive (welcome, take to its heart), because it does not see Him or know and recognize Him. But you know and recognize Him, for He lives with you [constantly] and will be in you." (John 14:17).

The Holy Spirit now dwells in the heart just as the dove, His symbol, descended and nestled on Jesus' head during His baptism. He has made His home on earth since the day of Pentecost. Throughout this dispensation, the church of Jesus Christ is the home of the Holy Spirit in the same way that heaven is the home of Jesus Christ.

The Scene In The Maternity Room Of The Holy Spirit

Every one of them was paying heed! There was a noise in heaven! It immediately gathered traction and loudness! Where was the sound which was accompanied by a wind — the sound of a mighty rushing wind coming from? It was thrusting, scrubbing, hollering, and as it descended, the mystical wind entered the maternity ward where the one hundred and twenty disciples were gathered with astonishment and unexpectedness! The mighty wind-like sound was a clear sign that it was coming from heaven. Typical winds blow from this or that quarter of the sky, but on the day of Pentecost, the wind descended from heaven itself: it was clearly from above. A normal rushing mighty wind would have been felt outside the room and would have most likely destroyed the house or injured the residents if it had been directed at any building.

The house in which they were gathered started convulsing! The mighty, rushing sound filled every corner of the room. The strong heavenly wind, however, filled but did not destroy the room and graced but did not depose the tarrying disciples. No one really fully understood what the emotions of the hundred and twenty were like, but they surely looked up to Jesus.

Were they afraid? Dreading? Despaired? Doubting? Scared? Worried? Nobody could tell. However, the disciples had been with Jesus of Miracles for three and a half years. Therefore, they might, at least, understand that the Holy Spirit's work in the Life of their Master was and still is, in a sense, the breath of God, and His power was and still is, in a special sense, the instantaneous power of God. The symbol means that, just as air, breath, and wind are crucial to man's survival, so is the Spirit of God crucial to spiritual survival.

The Holy Spirit initially quickens Christians. After that, He keeps us alive. He cultivates, expands, and perfects our inner life. The Spirit of God is the breath of the nostrils of the Christians. The heavenly breath of Pentecost was meant to revitalize the disciples as well as quicken them. The mighty rushing wind quickly cleared away all earth-generated damps and gasses. It roused the disciples and prepared them for Jesus Christ's future work. The disciples drank deeply from the heavenly life. They were enlivened, stimulated, and bestirred. They were overcome with a holy exuberance because the Holy Spirit filled them.

They were girting with that power and rose to a higher moral way of life than they had known before. Suddenly, fire tongues appeared in front of their transfixed gaze. Their faces were lit up by its hopping, bursting, consuming, and ignition glory. And each of the disciples possessed a blazing tongue that burned brightly on their heads. Tongues of flame on each of the one hundred and twenty heads denote a personal visitation to each of the chosen companies' minds and hearts. The fires did not come to consume them because the flaming tongue injured none of the disciples.

There is no danger in Jesus' visits to Christians who have been prepared for His arrival. They see God, and their lives are spared.

They feel His fires but are not ingested. Thus, a Christian gets prepared and cleansed for such fellowship with God.

The purpose of the fire was to demonstrate to the disciples that the Holy Spirit would illuminate them just as fire does:

"But when He, the Spirit of Truth (the Truth-giving Spirit) comes, He will guide you into all the truth (the whole, full Truth). He shall lead you into all truth." (John 16:13).

They were no longer to be inexperienced students but to be teachers in Jerusalem, Judea, Samaria, and of the nations whom they were to disciple to Christ: thus, the Spirit of light was upon them:

"But (ability, efficiency, and might) when the Holy Spirit has come upon you, and you shall be My witnesses in Jerusalem and all Judea and Samaria and to the ends (the very bounds) of the earth. (Acts 1:8).

But fire does more than give light; it inflames, and the flames that sat upon each of the disciples showed them that they were to be ablaze with love, zealous with thirst for souls, and self-sacrificing with fire. They were, thus, to go out among the people, speaking not in the cold tongue of deliberate logic. Instead, with burning tongues of passionate pleading, He persuaded and entreated people to come to Jesus Christ in order to live. The fire represented motivation. God was about to make the disciples speak under divine influence, as the Holy Spirit of God gave them utterance.

The emblem on the disciples' heads was not just fire but a tongue of fire. God desires a speaking Christian and a speaking church, not a Christian and a church that fight with a gun — we have nothing to do with that weapon. But God desires a Christian and a church with a sword protruding from their mouth and whose sole weapon is the proclamation of the gospel of Jesus Christ.

Beloved, may all Christians fully understand the importance of the two Pentecost symbols. May the rushing wind and the tongue of fire perpetually rest on every Christian. May a fire burn progressively within us to destroy our many weaknesses, a holy sacrificial flame to make Christians whole, burnt offerings unto God, a never-failing flame of zeal for God and devotion to the cross!

Hallelujah!

The Essence Of Pentecost

There were about five key days in the commencement of Christianity: the birthday of Jesus, the day of His death, the day of His resurrection, the day of His ascension, and the day of Pentecost. Each of those days was defined and distinguished by incredible wonders.

Everything has significance in the Christian religion. Christianity, like PENTECOST, is a way of life that is always developing and replicated in the heart of every Christian. The Pentecost that Christians often remember is the one recounted in the Acts of the Apostles:

"And when the day of Pentecost had fully come, they were all assembled together in one placed..." (Acts 2:1).

Pentecost, on the other hand, had a long history. It was the second of three Mosaic feasts, occurring fifty days following Passover. The Passover commemorates the day when God told the Israelites in Egypt:

"...when I see the blood, I will pass over you." (Exodus 12:13).

On the morning after the Passover Sabbath, the Israelites brought the wave-sheaf of their barley harvest which was waved before God in metaphor that every product of the earth and every fruit of man's work came from God and belonged to God. The feast was originally known as the Farmers' Festival of the First Fruits. Seven weeks after the barley harvest and the feast of first fruits for all harvests, especially the wheat harvest which was then in full bloom: that was Pentecost.

Pentecost later came to represent Sinai. On that day, the Ten Commandments, commonly known as the Decalogue, were read aloud in the congregations. Following that, the sons renewed the vows made by their fathers. Pentecost was, thus, regarded as the period of the giving of the law in the Jewish religion. And when the law was revealed on Sinai, there was a tremendous display of power. Therefore, it is not surprising that on the Day of Pentecost, when the Gospel was given, there was some spectacular manifestation of the divine presence. Thus, we expect the Holy Spirit to continue working amazing miracles and wonders at the beginning of the Gospel in every heart.

While Pentecost can be considered a historical event, everything spiritual and important about it persists. God's opened heavens, as they were on the day of Pentecost, are kept open. So that the church of today can have a continual Pentecost, the Holy Spirit continues to fall onto waiting hearts in the form of an invisible "wind" and "spirit".

Pentecost was not a separate and independent event. It was not anything separate from all that happened throughout Jesus' ministry. Considering them in their historical order and significance, we see how the value of the one depends on the truth of the other. The day of the ascension is wonderful because of Jesus Christ's virgin birth, crucifixion, and resurrection. The day of Pentecost was only facilitated and significant by Jesus Christ's ascension to the place of dignity and power.

Pentecost marked the culmination of an endless period of redemption work. It was the pinnacle of the divine's descent into humankind. It marked a turning point in history, the significance of which we are only now understanding.

The coming of Jesus Christ in the flesh, and the coming of the Holy Spirit, are the two fundamental events in historical Christianity; the former being the beginning of God's specific manifestation to man, and the latter the means of the former's continuation and fulfillment. The coming of the Holy Spirit marks the end of Jesus Christ's coming. It changed the course of history; it elevated the world into the heavens, infused it with God's life, and hid within its heart a force that contains the power and promise of its total salvation.

Christians of all times will not honor Pentecost if we refer to the day as simply a historical occurrence. The world has never been the same since the advent of the Holy Spirit. A glorious perspective has been obtained that should not be lost. The world should keep doing its best.

The truth for which Pentecost stands must be emphasized now more than ever to oppose any ideology against the concept of God. There is no more pressing responsibility that modern Christians have than to study the issues of crucial importance that have gathered around the blessed event of Pentecost.

Pentecost has a timeless quality to it. There is also something progressive about it: it has spanned centuries. Christians may not be able to see the outward manifestation of Pentecost with tongues and fire resting on their heads. But the Pentecost fire remains unchanged and unfading. The same is blazing on the Christian soul's inner altar.

Unfortunately, many Christians seek a new Pentecost and its power that is already in them. But it still impacts us today. And it will have an impact on others tomorrow. In a Christian, the Holy Spirit outlives everything in the world in majesty and power.

I, therefore, humbly call on every Christian to understand what Pentecost means regarding the fulfillment of God's purpose in their life, the place it occupies in the process of redemptive development; and what it means to the contemporary world.

"Christianity, like PENTECOST,
is a way of life that is always
developing and replicated in
the heart of every Christian".

CHAPTER 08

WHAT PENTECOST IS NOT

For all that Pentecost has offered humanity, it is fair to argue that a Christian should not regard Pentecost as an event but as a relationship that must be pursued at all costs. To help us understand what Pentecost is, I would want to start with what *Pentecost Is Not* because, in many cases, the opposite of a good thing increases its value.

In January 2014, charismatic Christian leaders gathered in Toronto to commemorate the 20th anniversary—a special conference held at Catch the Fire, commonly known as the Toronto Blessing. The Toronto Blessing, as dubbed by British newspapers, was a revival and ensuing phenomenon that began in January 1994 at the Toronto Airport Vineyard Church, now known as the Toronto Airport Christian Fellowship, a charismatic church in Toronto, Canada.

It has also been called the Father's Blessing. The blessing is noted for exuberant worship, including falling, slaying, resting in the Spirit, laughter, shaking, screaming, and crying. After the beginning of 1994, Church leaders in Britain began to speak of God's new move. At least 4,000 churches from diverse Christian denominations claimed to have been impacted by the Toronto Blessing. While the congregants testified about a very real blessing from God, many others were and continued to be skeptical. Many

Christians regarded the manifestations associated with God's move as strange if not weird.

I shall not speak for either side of the argument. However, I believe it is equally true that God's power which is also the Holy Spirit's power can manifest itself in Christians while none of them laugh, scream, shake, cry, jerk, jump, slay, or fall under the Spirit's influence.

Therefore, it would be dangerous for any Christian to absolutely ascribe every laugh, shake, shout, and cry at church or a prayer meeting to the Holy Spirit. Because human psychology and God's engagement with it are complex subjects, a Christian's laughter, shaking, screaming, and crying during church service can have various reasons. However, because of occurrences like those and many others, Jesus has generously endowed His Church with a plethora of "HELPS" so that we might discern and carefully determine whether His Spirit is at work or whether other spirits are:

"So God has appointed some in the church [for His own use]: first apostles (special messengers); second prophets (inspired preachers and expounders); third teachers; then wonder-workers; then those with ability to heal the sick; helpers; administrators; [speakers in] different (unknown) tongues." (1 Corinthians 12:28).

Emotionalism Mistaken As The Holy Spirit's Manifest Power

Amma may be called the iron Christian; she was an eleven-year-old stern and brave girl who flinched not to deliver her Master's message at all hazards. It was fitting that such a young girl should be raised up at that time because a false prophet Ampofo of Bibiani was a man of domineering spirit, superstitious to the extreme, and resolute in carrying out his selfish purpose, controlling countless weak Christians with imperial lies and false doctrine.

He had persuaded many adult Christians who were experiencing marital, financial and health issues that the only way to solve their problems was for a deceased person to manifest through them causing them to laugh, scream, tremble, cry, jerk, jump, and get "slain" under the power of the Holy Spirit. And although many Christians opposed the prophet's new doctrine, none could stand up to this wolf in sheep's clothing until Amma returned home for vacation from a boarding school. Amma went to the false prophet's prayer camp at the invitation of her Sunday school teacher. She witnessed how practically everyone at the camp laughed, yelled, shook, cried, jerked, jumped, and got "slain" as soon as the prayer session began. Amma looked everywhere for a complete and adequate explanation of the Holy Spirit's operations.

Thank God, Providence threw at Amma a sermon preached at a Holy Ghost convention under the theme "Life Abundance in the Holy Spirit" by Apostle Professor Opoku Onyinah (Former Chairman of The Church of Pentecost). Amma overheard the apostle say:

"The Holy Spirit who lives in a Christian will not abandon His position for any other spirit to conduct His work."

Amma's experience at the Bibiani Prayer Camp struck a chord with her right away. She perceived Bibiani's false prophet and all of his camp workers as traitors to the Christian God. And, armed with what she had learned about the Holy Spirit throughout the sermon, Amma dared the false prophet to make the utmost mischief with his false doctrine. That lone eleven-year-old courageous soul stemmed the terrifying flood of disguised necromancy standing strong like a rock in mid-current.

Even as one lion scatters a flock of sheep, Amma and a few others who had come to their senses were more than a match for the Bibiani false prophet and his workers. Amma, through the power of the Holy Spirit, exposed the false prophet of Bibiani as a liar and an impostor. And then, being the logical thinker that she is, she arrived at the logical conclusion:

"The Holy Spirit who lives in a Christian will not abandon His position for any other spirit to conduct His work."

After a few experiences as a Christian in which over 80% of a congregation embraced such false beliefs as the false prophet of Bibiani, I proposed one particular remedy at the beginning. When you meet someone who believes their problems will not be solved unless they laugh, shout, shake, cry, jerk, jump, get "slain", or fall under the influence of the Spirit, simply ask them to tell you their problem. It is almost always beneficial for the depressed to share their spiritual predicament with others.

Emotionalism, which causes people to laugh, shout, shake, cry, jerk, jump, get "slain", and so on, must always be avoided; it has been and continues to be a pandemic in Christianity. I humbly pray that the Holy Spirit will fill us and make us ready to be a help to everyone at every time.

*"In everyday life, our thoughts
are preoccupied with the things
that are most essential to
our survival."*

CHAPTER 09

NOT A WHOLESALE SALVATION

When I was a little girl, my Dad gave me a strict rule never to share with anyone what happens in our family at home. But when I started attending school, I realized the rule was quite different for some children at their home. In my class, I always overheard a guileless little child telling out all they had seen with their father and mother. Those children shared even the innermost secrets of the family with naivete and sweetness. My teacher, hearing the talking children, sometimes laughed heartily as he listened to how those little-talker-tongued children laid everything bare.

But then, when I first read about Jesus Christ's behaving like a chatter, I heartily laughed.

"I tell the things which I have seen and learned at My Father's side, and your actions also reflect what you have heard and learned from your father." (John 8:38).

I wish I could express to the fullest my admiration in words, but I cannot, for it is very lovely that Jesus Christ would behave in a good-natured taleteller to us.

Jesus Christ, the beloved Holy Son, lived and taught with all of His life like a child telling what they had seen at home. He came to share with the world His Father's love and plans. He reveals to us that which He has seen with the Father as a child by becoming our childlike nature in all our immaturity. He revealed to the world the innermost thoughts of God by giving His life. He came to share with us, the younger members of the family who are made so by grace, everything He had seen with the Father. That was THE PLAN OF SALVATION.

The Godhead, the Father, the Son, and the Holy Spirit, with wisdom, put to work to devise means by which sinners who have been banished from Him may be restored. Jesus Christ speaks of it thus:

"All whom My Father gives (entrusts) to Me will come to Me; and the one who comes to Me I will most certainly not cast out [I will never, no never, reject one of them who comes to Me]." (John 6:37).

Therefore, the prison deliverance comes to everyone by promise. It is salvation according to promise. God has promised that every sinner shall be saved on the plan of salvation (John 3:16). It is not the result of anything anyone does. No sinner ever deserved salvation; it is not the result of a bargain between a sinner and God. No! Jesus Christ came to bring to all those who believe in Him a complete deliverance from the walls of the prison. Anyone who believes in Jesus is forgiven; the very moment they believe, all their transgressions are blotted out. And from that moment, they are just in the sight of God. *"Being justified by faith, we have peace with God through Jesus Christ our Lord."* Having believed, we become, at once, children of God, children of the Most High, and since God will never cast away His children nor reject those whom He has loved; they are saved, and saved eternally. We were slaves before and deserved the lash and felt it; but we are children now and are no longer under the law but under grace. The principle which guides the saved now is not *"This do, and thou shalt live"*, but this — *"I am saved, and now I love to serve my God"*. You do not work for wages and expect to win a reward by merit; we are saved people and have all that we need; for Christ is ours, and Christ is all. How a higher principle burns within our bosom than self-salvation, we love God and are no longer selfish.

It is, thus, evident that the way to be saved is to come to Jesus Christ. He is a Person, a living Person, full of power to save. Jesus Christ has not placed His salvation in sacraments. He has not placed it in any human being: priests, presidents, husbands, wives, or friends. He has kept salvation in Himself. And anyone who wants to have salvation must come to Jesus Christ. He is the one Source and Fountain of eternal mercy. There is no getting it by going round about Him or only going near to Him. Everyone must come to Jesus Christ. Personal contact must be established between Jesus Christ and a sinner's Spirit.

The Only But One Way

In everyday life, our thoughts are preoccupied with the things that are most essential to our survival. During the COVID-19 pandemic, no one murmured that the subject of "Quarantine", "Social distancing", "Mask", "Vaccine", and "COVID Test" were frequently on the lips of the people of the world. It was because everyone felt that the subject was critical to the general public. Therefore, no one grumbled despite hearing those lines in constant voluble remarks. We even regularly read and watched pieces about it in the press.

Jesus Christ made the same case throughout His earthly mission and constantly brought up the topic of regeneration to everyone. He said:

"...I assure you, most solemnly I tell you, that unless a person is born again (anew, from above), he cannot ever see (know, be acquainted with, and experience) the kingdom of God" (John 3:3).

The *"The kingdom of God"*, what is it? I can say the kingdom of God is Heaven without using a single superfluous theological term. However, the great God has always had a kingdom in this world. In the olden times, He set up a kingdom among His people Israel to whom He gave laws and statutes. But God is also King over all the world:

"The earth and all its fullness are the Lord's; the globe and all who dwell in it." (Psalm 24:1 KJV).

God has a kingdom in this world, but it is too much neglected and forgotten by men:

"...the God of the whole earth He is called." (Isaiah 54:5).

It is because when Satan, the Prince of Darkness, was cast from heaven to the earth, he established his kingdom here on earth and continues to have dominion over man.

Every human being, from their mother's womb, enters straight into the kingdom of Sin, also known as the prison of sinners, where Satan is the king. *"Ye were the servants of sin."* (Romans 6:17). Everyone in the kingdom of Sin is not all alike subjects of Satan, but they are all under bondage. Sin has its liveried servants.

But it pleased God to lay all the world's Sins on Jesus Christ's cross. The Father made His begotten Son a scapegoat for all His other children and took their sins away. Some of the contexts of Jesus Christ's telltale is that God the loving Father has a sword. The Father, through His Son Jesus Christ, is calling every sinner to abandon the kingdom of Sin and come into God's kingdom of Righteousness. If a sinner refuses to heed the calling, God the Father will "whet His sword".

So, every human being has a universal responsibility to abandon the kingdom of Satan and enter the kingdom of God where Jesus Christ is the King. In the kingdom of God, all the subjects learn to order their life according to divine law. In God's kingdom, there is the highest liberty from wearing His yoke.

We can only enter into the kingdom of God by being born again of God's Spirit. A new birth is, in fact, more than a change; it is a creation. Regeneration is a great deal more than a reformation of life or a becoming religious. Jesus Christ did not say: "You must be washed, you must be improved, you must be elevated," But He said: "You must be born."

It is not enough that a sinner's present life, as they already possess, should be renovated. It is not enough for the existing nature to receive fresh vigor and a new tone. Every human being must and should heed to the call *"Ye must be born again"*: they have to receive a new life. And no improving the present life will suffice in its stead.

In that new birth, a convert finds in Jesus Christ eternal life. We learn to submit ourselves to Jesus Christ. John the Baptist pictured Jesus Christ in many lights and characters. John pointed Jesus Christ out as the great moral example, the Founder of a higher form of life, and the Great Teacher of holiness and love.

"The next day, John saw Jesus coming to him and said, Look! There is the Lamb of God, who takes away the sin of the world!" (John 1:29).

God has appointed Jesus Christ heir of all things.

"Kiss the Son [pay homage to Him in purity], lest He be angry, and you perish in the way, for soon shall His wrath be kindled. O blessed (happy, fortunate, and to be envied) are all those who seek refuge and put their trust in Him." (Psalm 2:12).

So, to summarize what Jesus said about entering the kingdom of God, I say that anyone who will not be born again cannot enter heaven. There is an actual impossibility in their nature, which prevents them from enjoying any of heaven's bliss.

Every life is prefaced by rib birth. It is so natural we are born; it is so spiritual we are born again. Except a person is naturally born, they cannot enter the prison of sinners. Except a person is born again, they cannot enter the Kingdom of God. Birth is both the humble portal through which we enter the realm of evil and the lofty portal through which we reach the Kingdom of God.

The Christian first heaven is a state that is made in them on earth. It is made in their heart by God's Spirit within us. And we cannot enjoy the things of heaven unless God the Spirit renews us and causes us to be born again.

Similar to how it is physically impossible for a goat to ever lecture on organic chemistry, an unborn human cannot enter into the kingdom of God.

*"Regeneration is a great deal
more than a reformation of
life or a becoming religious."*

THE UNIVERSALITY OF THE HUMAN JOB IS TO SAVE SOULS

On February 6, 2023, at 4.17 am, local time, wreaking havoc and killing tens of thousands of people, the first of many earthquakes and aftershocks devastated cities in Turkey and Syria. A search, rescue, and relief operations supported by dozens of neighborhood organizations, as well as a continual stream of volunteers, quickly began working. Given how large the work was, international organizations promptly sent aid to Turkey and Syria to assist them in coping with the powerful quakes. Additionally, the U.S. provided aid workers and supplies to help find survivors. Rescuers kept working around the clock for hours, days, and weeks in an effort to finding more survivors among the rubbles. In Kahramanmaras, after the magnitude 7.8 and 7.6 earthquakes, the majority of the city center, including homes, businesses, banks, and markets, was reduced to rubbles. Search and rescue crews battled through mounds of debris in dire search of dying victims.

With more than 21,500 people dead, subzero temperatures and heaps of rubbles, there was no or little prospect of discovering many more survivors. Nevertheless, amid the devastation were stories of tenacity and survival; of lives miraculously rescued even after spending days trapped beneath the debris. Al Jazeera's Resul Serdar, reporting from a rescue site in Kahramanmaras, relayed:

"Another body was pulled out from under the rubble, and he was alive … 110 hours later. An ambulance now took him to the hospital. And there is another [man] now; they are digging for him."

According to the correspondent, rescuers were initially unsure if the second man was still alive:

"But the hope here at this moment is very high that a second person – maybe minutes later – could be pulled out from under the rubble, and that he is also alive, 110 hours later."

A three-and-a-half-year-old girl was also rescued alive from the same rescue site's wreckage just a few hours earlier.

After being trapped alive under the wreckage of a collapsed building in the town of Kirikhan for 104 hours, Zeynep Kahraman, 40, was found alive. German rescue personnel carried her into an ambulance on a stretcher.

"Now I believe in miracles" Steven Bayer, the leader of the international search and rescue team said at the site. You can see the people crying and hugging each other. It's such a huge relief that this woman came out so fit under such conditions. It's an absolute miracle."

Eyup Ak, 60, was found alive in the wreckage of a fallen building in the southern Turkish province of Adiyaman on Friday 104 hours after becoming trapped by the earthquake. After being rescued, Ak was taken to the hospital on a stretcher. 103 hours after the initial earthquake, Murat Vural, 66, was found in the Islahiye area of the province of Gaziantep. Following 10 hours of hard work, the police and members of Turkey's National Medical Rescue Team (UMKE) successfully removed Vural from the rubbles.

After 103 hours, Azerbaijani teams in Kahramanmaras managed to save a 15-year-old Syrian girl. Also, a thre-and-a-half-year-old girl in Hatay was rescued from the wreckage 103 hours after the main earthquake. 33-year-old Mustafa Sahin Sami was saved by UMKE and the police teams in the Elbistan area of Kahramanmaras province 102 hours after the initial earthquake. He was extracted from a seven-story building's rubbles after a 12-hour operation by many teams.

According to the rescuers, after spending 101 hours buried in the rubble, 6 people were rescued from a collapsed building in Iskenderun, Turkey. According to Murat Baygul, a search and rescue worker, the six people—all relatives—were able to stay alive by huddling together in a little pocket that was left inside the fallen building. 101 hours after the initial earthquake, a miner crew from Zonguldak saved Ihlas Ayaz and her son.

2 sisters, ages 15 and 13, were rescued from the ruins in the province of Kahramanmaras. The 15-year-old and her younger sister received medical care while confined for a combined 99 and 101 hours. Naim Bayasli, 32, was rescued from the wreckage of a collapsed building in Hatay province by an Uzbek rescue team after being stuck there for 100 hours.

A family, including a 1-year-old girl, was rescued from the wreckage of a fallen building after 96 hours. The infant's mother, father, brother, and uncle were among the family members. After being stranded for 96 hours, they were rescued in the Antakya neighborhood of Hatay. 96 hours after the earthquake, Fatma Karus, a 26-year-old Syrian woman, was rescued by the rescuers in Kahramanmaras.

The rescuers in Gaziantep rescued a 17-year-old boy from the basement where he had been held for 94 hours. As he was being placed into an ambulance and while embracing his mother and everyone who had knelt down to kiss and hug him, the teenager exclaimed: *"Thank God you arrived!"* As he was being taken out, a group of friends and family members cheered and cheered him on and shed happy tears. The teenager claimed he was compelled to quench his thirst by drinking his own urine. I was able to survive that way. A rescuer who only went by the name of Yasemin told him:

"I have a son just like you. I swear to you, I have not slept for four days. I swear I did not sleep; I was trying to get you out."

After being trapped for 90 hours, a 10-day-old baby and its mother were discovered alive in Hatay. At the last minute, 2 more people were rescued from the rubble: a 5-year-old child and her Father. A 7-year-old boy and his 32-year-old father, Ozan Ramazan Guclu, were found alive in Kahramanmaras after 89 hours. After 88 hours, rescuers in Adyaman, Turkey, were able to rescue from the ruins of a six-story structure two siblings, ages 7 and 14.

*"It is so natural we are born;
it is so spiritual we are born again."*

Every Soul Matters

A video from the DHA news agency shows rescuers in Istanbul stretching between two large concrete slabs and calling to a dog who was trapped as the disaster's death toll passed 50,000. One rescuer was heard asking while crouched within a tiny crevice in the wreckage of the structure, *"Is he coming?"* One of the rescuers appealed to the canine, *"Aleks, come, my pet. Congratulations, my son!"* The dog was then seen being hugged by the rescuers and being given water. The dog appeared to be conscious and in good health. Teams from a regional government in central Turkey sent Aleks, the dog to Haytap, a Turkish organization for animal protection in the city of Antakya. In Antakya, one of the cities completely destroyed by the disaster, rescue personnel rescued hundreds of trapped cats, dogs, rabbits, and birds beloved by the residents.

After every miraculous rescue, a local reporter is quoted by the privately-owned DHA agency as saying: *"Every living thing matters to us, human beings or animals"*. The rescuers could not have said it better. For God delights in those who do good to animals.

"Good people are good to their animals; but bad people kick and abuse them" (Proverbs 12:10 MSG).

All life is not the same as I have previously stated, and neither is all flesh. Man, animal, and plant life may exhibit some similarities to one another, but they are not the same. Taste, hunger, and instinct are things that only animals possess; they do not exist in the universe in which plants grow.

Although, we, humans tend to think of ourselves as a unique species, it turns out that we share many characteristics with animals. Science journal research claims that the arrangement of katydid ears is quite similar to that of human ears. In order to magnify vibrations, it has eardrums and lever systems. It has an information-gathering vesicle filled with fluid where sensory cells await to provide information to the nervous system.

To name a few, as far as we can tell, humans dominate the field of language. However, even elephants may learn to imitate our voices. Researchers claim that an Asian elephant housed in a zoo in South Korea has mastered the use of its trunk and neck to imitate human voices and words. The elephant can communicate in Korean and can say "hi", "good", "no", "sit down", and "lay down".

Animals have the capacity to breathe, move, communicate, and feel pain, hunger, and emotion. And the reason is that they contain a component known as the soul. However, human life is far superior to an animal's, just as an animal's life is greatly superior to the experience and apprehension of a field flower. Humans have a mental life that takes us into a world very different from a simple animal's. No animal possesses the ability to assess, predict, imagine, invent, or carry out moral deeds.

The rescuers in Turkey and all other countries work for God. They swept in the dust looking for the physically lost human beings. They held lights at night shedding their feeble rays as far as they could. Many were, somewhat, weary. Without a doubt, many of them were scratched by many a briar. They were tired after their many desperate leaps over hill and dale. But their souls were refreshed by looking upon some of the results of their toil. They forgot all their weariness and began to chant and share in the joy of all the people gathered. Those rescuers in Turkey and Syria sought physical human beings. However, they imitated the Great, Good, Chief Shepherd Jesus Christ, who seeks after lost souls.

And when He finds one soul before the throne of God on high, they make merry over the souls that have been saved. In pursuit of the same purpose, I take up the expressive figure of the preciousness of the soul to address myself to everyone who has the chance to read my writings.

"Birth is both the humble portal through which we enter the realm of evil and the lofty portal through which we reach the Kingdom of God."

CHAPTER 10

Evangelism Global Positioning Systems (GPS)

Jesus did not commission His disciples to create a gospel or its GPS. Instead, He gave them His Gospel and laid out their approach to spreading the good news.

Christians who do not obey the command "Go!" are miscreants and traitors. However, there is plenty of room for introspection regarding obeying Jesus Christ's command to "Go!"

Where

Jesus, when He opened the scriptures to His disciples before His accession, told them that repentance and remission of sins should be preached in His name among all nations.

"And that repentance [with a view to and as the condition of] forgiveness of sins should be preached in His name to all nations, beginning from Jerusalem." (Luke 24:47).

So, they had the divine warrant for missions. They were no speculations or enthusiastic dreams: they were matters of divine command. The disciples had marching orders that said:

"And He said to them, Go into all the world and preach and publish openly the good news (the Gospel) to every creature [of the whole human race]." (Mark 16:15).

Thus, Christians are to preach the gospel everywhere: missions are to be universal. All nations need the preaching of the word. The gospel is a remedy for every human ill among all the races that live upon the face of the earth. We ought to preach the gospel to every creature, for it is written that it was meant to be so. Every Christian, according to their ability and opportunity, should tell everyone they meet the story of sin forgiveness through Jesus Christ's death, the Mediator's sacrifice. Jesus Christ commands us to proclaim to all creatures repentance for sin and faith in Him.

Preaching The Three "Rs"

The content of a Christian's preaching can be described in various ways, but when preaching the gospel to a dying world, it consists of three elements: *ruin, repentance,* and *remission* of sins.

Ruin

Adam's disobedience ruined humanity. However, Jesus Christ's obedience resulted in repentance and remission of sins. Through deception, Satan persuaded Adam and Eve to violate God's explicit command, the compliance of which was a requirement of their joy. As a result of their disobedience, God drove Adam and Eve out of the Garden of Eden making them subject to the judgment of death, and sentenced them to unending sorrow. The entire human race became susceptible to the dreadful consequences of Adam's fall due to our relationship with him as our federal head and representative.

Thus, human beings' faces have been turned away from God since the terrible day when Adam and Eve disobeyed God's commandment, and we have all been guilty of the same great sin. Humanity stood with our backs to "Repentance and Remission" on the downhill road to "Ruin" which leads to eternal death.

Repentance

What every sinner needs is to turn about, for that is the meaning of the word "Repentance" — Right-about-turn.

Christians interpret the word "repentance" as a "change of mind". Undoubtedly, the word denotes a change of thought, but in its biblical context, it suggests a change of mind of an uncommon type. It is not the same as what people mean when they say they change their minds a thousand times a day; rather, it is a profound change of mind.

Gospel repentance is a monumental change of mind, such as has never been wrought in any human except by the Holy Spirit. It is a change that concerns the human mind, affections, and spirit. It is not a physical manipulation, as some people believe, in which God changes people by force and rolls them over like a stone. It is not so. God operates upon humans as humans, not as blocks of wood. God speaks to them, instructs them, reveals the truth to them, encourages them to hope, and graciously influences them for good.

Thus, through Christians, God preaches repentance to demonstrate to the sinner that they should experience sorrow and desire to quit the lifestyle they once liked. As a result, it becomes a Christian's responsibility to preach to the sinner nothing but repentance:

"Such [former] ages of ignorance God, it is true, ignored and allowed to pass unnoticed; but now He charges all people everywhere to repent (to change their minds for the better and heartily to amend their ways, with abhorrence of their past sins), Because He has fixed a day when He will judge the world righteously (justly) by a Man whom He has destined and appointed for that task, and He has made this credible and given conviction and assurance and evidence to everyone by raising Him from the dead." (Acts 17:30-31).

Every Christian must preach the acceptance of repentance. Nothing in repentance justifies God's favor in and of itself, but because of Jesus Christ's love, suffering, and death, God accepts sinners' repentances:

"He who covers his transgressions will not prosper, but whoever confesses and forsakes his sins will obtain mercy" (Proverbs 28:13).

When God accepts a sinner's repentance for the sake of His precious Son, He smiles upon the remorseful sinner and forgives their sins. When preaching the repentance gospel, Christians must highlight repentant motives. It is unsurprising to find many Christians who have simply repented out of dread of hell but have not repented of sin itself.

Many criminals become remorseful when they are sentenced to prison, and many murderers quickly become priests when they are scheduled to be executed in an electric chair or any other dreadful means. Such is not the repentance God seeks; He wants a sinner to repent not because of the penalty for sin but because their sin is against a loving God, a suffering sinless Savior, a righteous law, and a gentle gospel.

Genuine remorseful sinners repent of their sins against God, and they would do so even if there were no punishment. When they are forgiven, they repent of their sins more than ever before because they realize the evil of offending such a merciful God more plainly than ever before. A Christian must preach eternal repentance. Repentance is not a virtue to be practiced by the repented sinner only briefly or seldom at the commencement of their Christian journey; it is to accompany the repented sinner all the way to heaven. Faith and repentance are to be intimate friends on a Christian's journey all the way to heaven.

Repentance for our sins and trust in the merciful Sin Bearer is to be the theme of a Christian's life, and we are to preach that theme to sinners until they make it their theme.

REMISSION OF SIN

I have always associated the term "remission" with Apostle Paul. *"…and without shedding of blood is no remission." (Hebrews 9:22 KJV).* Many people may dislike the sound of the words "no remission". The phrase "no remission" is engraved permanently in a sinner's mind. From the day Adam fell until today, that has been the writing in every sinner's memory: "no remission".

The sacrificial death of Jesus Christ has removed the phrase "No Remission" from every Christian's memory. On the other hand, the sinner's memories are like a never-ending nightmare. The phrase is constantly on their minds.

The phrase, "No Remission", implies that someone is sinning, and that person is the focus of God's continuous anger. Undeniably, God is displeased with a sinner.

"...God is angry with the wicked every day." (Psalm 7:11).

Yet, He has compassionate regard for sinners as one of His creatures and does not want them to perish. God would infinitely prefer that the sinner turn to Him and live rather than regard him as impenitent.

Nature and Satan do very well to preach to the sinner that God has no pleasure for them. Satan makes sure that a sinner constantly reflects on the fact that God is angry with them. Although this is not the case, Satan makes several attempts to re-imprint in a Christian's memory the agonizing feeling of living under the sense of God's anger. So, in the case of a sinner, Satan uses every means imaginable to convince them that God will never forgive their sins and will be displeased with them even if they repent.

The third "R" of the three "Rs" addresses Satan's deception methods with sinners. When preaching the gospel to a sinner, a Christian must emphasize complete and permanent remission. We have to convey to the sinner that God does not provide forgiveness and then turn around and take it back. He is not a Father who can forgive a sinner's sins while punishing them.

Many Christians commit a grave mistake of separating the Godhead when preaching the gospel to a sinner. As a result, the sinner may believe that Jesus, the Son, is willing to save them, but God the Father is not.

They present God the Father as a Mighty Being full of anger, indignation, and justice and lacking in love because they are ignorant of the system of salvation. Such beliefs could never be more incorrect. Without a doubt, Jesus, the Son, saves the sinner, but the Father provided the Son to die for the sinner and chose the sinner in His grace's everlasting adoption. The Father blots out the sinner's sin; the Father accepts the sinner and adopts them into His family through Jesus Christ.

Jesus Christ, the Son and Savior could not save anyone without the Father, just as the Father could not save anyone without the Son, and rebirth would be impossible without the Holy Spirit. God delivers the sinner's soul from the pit of hell so that their life may see the light. God visits the sinner through His word, speaks, chastens, instructs, enlightens, consoles, renews, and saves. Thus, from first to last, God works all in all. Salvation is of the Lord; it is not of man, neither by man; neither is it of the will of man, nor of the flesh, nor of blood, nor of birth, but of the will of God. The purpose of God and the power of God work salvation from first to last.

A Christian should so preach the basic objective of remission as total forgiveness of sin—that it is removed once and for all. However, a sinner must be made aware that everyone who repents must hate, despise, and turn away from their sin, or God will not forgive that sinner's sin in the first place. A Christian should enlighten sinners about the origin of repentance, specifically, that Jesus Christ has been elevated to grant repentance and forgiveness of sins.

Repentance is a plant that never grows on the garbage heap of sinners.

For repentance to flourish in our souls, human nature must be changed when the Holy Spirit sows it (repentance) in our nature. Thus, every sinner who believes in Jesus Christ is made righteous before God through Him having sin taken away by God. We are justified because of the faith we have in Jesus Christ:

"Therefore, since we are justified (acquitted, declared righteous, and given a right standing with God) through faith, let us [grasp the fact

that we] have [the peace of reconciliation to hold and to enjoy] peace with God through our Lord Jesus Christ (the Messiah, the Anointed One)." (Romans 5:1).*

Thus, every Christian and every Christian church must preach repentance as a fruit of the Spirit which causes a notorious sinner to not only have a "righteous" character, but also, to become the substance known as "righteousness".

Glory At The End Of The Destination

In many cases, the beginning of the godly and the upright and their work may be quite modest, and their ultimate end will be drastically great:

"Mark the perfect man, and behold the upright: for the end of that man is peace" (Psalm 37:37 KJV).

Evil news may appear to begin well and respectfully, but they end tragically. The path and GPS of evil news are downward, from its bright heights to its dark deep valleys, the massiveness it assumes when it claims to be an angelic message, and the decisiveness that it reveals to be a Satanic message.

No, not with good news (Gospel)! The gospel's beginning may be small, but its ultimate end is gloriously great. Jesus Christ planned the route of the gospel in the same way that a shining light sheds a few wavering beams at first, fights the darkness, and shines more and more until the perfect day. Jesus Christ did not leave it up to His disciples to decide where to begin preaching His gospel, but instead, directed them to begin in Jerusalem:

"… that repentance and remission of sin should be preached in His name among all nations, beginning at Jerusalem." (Luke 24:47 KJV).

When giving the commission to His disciples on this occasion, Jesus Christ had in mind some Old Testament passages; albeit, He did not quote them directly:

"And said to them, Thus it is written that the Christ (the Messiah) should suffer and on the third day rise from (among) the dead..." (Luke 24:46).

Fulfilment Of Old Testament Prophesies

The prophet Isaiah, who prophesied about the birth of Jesus Christ, appeared to be well-versed in His ministry and afterlife:

"...out of Zion shall come forth the law, and the word of the Lord from Jerusalem." (Isaiah 2:3 KJV).

Thus, if Isaiah's prophecy concerning the conception and birth of Jesus did not fail, his second prophecy about the preaching of the gospel beginning in Jerusalem had to come to pass. Joel, the second minor Old Testament prophet, prophesied about the descent of the Holy Spirit and the start of the evangelism GPS of Jesus Christ's disciples:

"...for in Mount Zion and in Jerusalem shall be deliverance;" (Joel 2:32 KJV).

Joel also added that:

"The Lord will thunder and roar from Zion and utter His voice from Jerusalem..." (Joel 3:16).

Obadiah, the fourth minor prophet, joined his voice to the GPS of the gospel, but his was directly regarding the pioneers of the gospel:

"And deliverers shall go up on Mount Zion to rule and judge..." (Obadiah 1:21).

Obadiah spoke about saviors who became so by proclaiming the Savior Jesus Christ. Speaking about the gospel's GPS, Zechariah, the eleventh minor prophet who was full of visions but not imaginative, said:

"And it shall be in that day, that living waters shall go out from Jerusalem..." (Zachariah 14:8).

The prophet then explained the path of those waters in his vision till they reached the Dead Sea and sweetened its waters. I cannot imagine what Christianity would have been like if the disciples had begun preaching the gospel from Judea, possibly close to Jerusalem. But, as Jesus had clearly instructed, they began in Jerusalem.

Throughout His life, Jesus Christ was insistent that the Old Testament be fulfilled to the word. The Faithful God who had prophesied through the prophets where the gospel would begin, who would be the first to preach it, and who would be the first to hear it, had to keep His word and perform. The GPS of the gospel demonstrates the abundance of God's grace. In Jesus' day, the inhabitants of Jerusalem had not pursued the gospel, nor had they pled for the grace of a gospel, nor had they longed for freedom from spiritual shackles. They were not even born during the time of the prophet Isaiah who prophesied about them:

"He shall come as a Redeemer to Zion and to those in Jacob (Israel) who turn from transgression, says the Lord;" (Isaiah 59:20).

God promised that the gospel would be preached in Jerusalem regardless of their attitude and behavior. The promise came to the unsolicited, the un-purchased, and the unconsidered people of the gospel that preaching the gospel would begin with them. The birth of the gospel in Jerusalem demonstrates God's grace in that He provides a promise before the sinner realizes their need or seeks a Savior.

When God makes a perfect grace promise, He does not suggest to the recipient: *"If you do this or that, I will do such and such."* But God appears and declares:

"And I will feed them that oppress thee with their own flesh...and all flesh shall know that I the LORD am thy Savior and thy Redeemer, the mighty One of Jacob." (Isaiah 49:26 KJV).

"The purpose of God and the power of God work salvation from first to last."

Facts

Jesus Christ commanded His disciples to begin preaching His gospel in Jerusalem because it was in Jerusalem that the events that comprise the gospel transpired. Jesus Christ was betrayed, arrested, scourged, humiliated, mocked, crucified, buried, died, rose again, and ascended into heaven. All of the events in the gospel took place in Jerusalem or close by. Imagine Jesus Christ told His disciples not to say anything at Jerusalem but to go to Samaria and begin preaching there. The GPS of the gospel and the disciple's actions would have raised red flags. The nobility of the gospel would not have looked nearly so powerful if He had not first commanded the disciples to preach His resurrection before the elders, the scribes, the priests, the Sadducees, and the Pharisees.

Based on the miracles at Golgotha during His crucifixion, the elders and many of Jesus' enemies may have been persuaded that He would resurrect as He had hinted while still alive. They bribed the soldiers to say otherwise, but they knew Jesus had resurrected:

"And when they [the chief priests] had gathered with the elders and had consulted together, they gave a sufficient sum of money to the soldiers; And said, Tell people, His disciples came at night and stole Him away while we were sleeping." (Matthew 28:12-13).

Jesus desired His disciples to preach the gospel on the streets of Jerusalem for a variety of other reasons. He had caused other Jerusalemites who had been crippled until He came to leap like a deer.

He multiplied fish and bread enough to feed thousands of men, women, and children. Jesus healed many Jerusalemites of severe and deadly illnesses. He raised dead children for their parents.

Thus, Jesus commanded His disciples to confront the tiger in his den and proclaim the gospel where, if it were false, it would have been met with resistance. He intended His disciples to be witnesses on the spot where they might be challenged if they lied and where people could come up and say:

"What you are preaching never happened; you are all deceivers like Him whom you follow."

When the disciples first began preaching the gospel in Jerusalem, they could point to places like the palaces of Annas, Caiaphas, Pilate, and Herod, where Jesus was paraded after being arrested at Gethsemane. They could call on witnesses from Jerusalem's streets who witnessed Jesus carry His cross. The disciples could take skeptics to the empty tombs of those who were resurrected after Jesus died. The disciples had so much evidence in Jerusalem to bring the gospel home to the Jerusalemites' consciences that they rejected the Beloved Son of God.

Thus, the inaugural preaching of Peter on the day of Pentecost had unconventional power: in addition to the power of the Holy Spirit, there was also a reason—that he was telling the people gathered of a murder that they had recently committed and could not deny: and when they saw their blunders, they turned to God with repentant hearts. Christianity has withstood the test of time and is, thus, deeply appreciated by its adherents.

Grace

The Jews of Jesus' days believed that they had dominance on God's grace; that God, who had selected their ancestors and pampered them with supernatural knowledge, would never deprive them of their advantages or advance others to similar privileges. They thought that God would almost certainly bless them above all other nations on the face of the planet.

Those Jews claimed to be Abraham's descendants, and Jesus Christ acknowledged their claim. However, Jesus knew the legitimacy of their claim to be Abraham's seed was based on flesh. Jesus had much to say in Abraham's credit at the time, but none could possibly surpass His remark to the braying unbelieving Jews in Jerusalem:

"Your forefather Abraham was extremely happy at the hope and prospect of seeing My day (My incarnation); and he did see it and was delighted." (John 8:56).

There was a lot of difference between the noble father Abraham and those Jews who claimed to be his children. They were always roaring like lions around the Lamb of God in Jerusalem, all eager to devour Him. Their hands were ever ready to pick up stones to assassinate the Lord of life and glory despite the fact that they were Abraham's descendants! Though they claimed to be the descendants of "God's friend" (Abraham), the Jews had always wanted to kill their father's Friend's (God) only begotten Son.

And a little time later, the same Jews, descended from the great father (Abraham), congregated in Jerusalem's street in front of Pilate's palace and shouted: "Crucify Him!" "Crucify Him! — that "Him" was the Son of their father's Friend.

After witnessing the unforgivable sins of the Jews against their beloved Master Jesus, He foresaw that some of His disciples would possibly hate the Jews. As a result, He instructed them:

"When you preach My gospel, begin with the Jews who despised Me." (Acts 1:8).

Jesus' command is a continuing mandate, and Christians should preach the gospel to Jews and Gentiles "to the Jew first." (Romans 1:16). As we say: "Ladies first"; then "Gentlemen", so "the Jew first." They have priority over other races, and Jesus will have them served first at the gospel dinner. God the Father, Jesus the Son, and God the Holy Spirit would have every Christian cherish the Jewish race that God appointed long ago and from whom Jesus Christ also descended. Although God's only begotten Son, Jesus, is a fleshly descendant of Abraham; and, like a loyal person, He prioritizes those He knows first and who know Him first.

Some Christians make disparaging remarks towards the Jewish people forgetting that their Master and Savior, Jesus Christ, is a Jew. Every Christian must understand that the Jews are the most glorified race in the world. They are the children of Abraham, God's Friend.

There are royals, princes, and princesses all over the world, yet they cannot trace their ancestors back to Abraham. However, the weakest Jew in the world is related directly to Jacob, Isaac, and Abraham. Instead of dismissing them, Jesus provided the gospel's GPS coordinates by instructing His disciples: "Begin from Jerusalem among the Jews."

The first address on the gospel GPS is "Begin at Jerusalem." As gospel drivers, we are to follow the gospel GPS and deliver the gospel first to the children of the father of faith, even Abraham. However, if they reject our package, we will be cleansed of their blood. But our mission will never be accomplished unless we stay on the road and follow the GPS all the way from the Jews to all the Gentiles.

Our Home, A Practical Jerusalem

Jerusalem was the capital city of Jesus' disciples' own homeland. It is not uncommon for a Christian to have to journey to heaven alone: salvation separates them from the midst of an ungodly family, and despite their godly example, prayers, and preaching, their family members remain unconverted. Thus, a lonely Christian, a colorful bird among others, pursues their lonely journey to the heavens.

Grace does not run in human blood, and rebirth has nothing to do with blood or human birth. But God, if He so desires, can win to Himself an entire family or a group through the conversion of one member of a household or a group of friends. God first calls a person and then uses them as a spiritual bait to attract into the gospel net the rest of the family; so, the God of Abraham becomes the God of Sarah, and then of Isaac and then of Jacob; the God of Priscilla becomes the God of Aquila; the God of Andronicus becomes the God of Junia; the God of Tryphena becomes the God of Tryphosa; etc.

When Christians first convert, they are filled with joy. They have the feeling that they are in a land of milk and honey, and they want everyone to taste their newfound sweetness. Their joy is infectious; it spreads more than a virus. The joyful Christian brings joy to others. They overflow with God's blessings for others.

The impact of a true Christian is first felt at home. They return home to their own family as a converted person, and the family members immediately notice the difference. True converted Christians tell their loved ones about what Jesus has done for them. Even if they tell their experience, those with whom the Christian interacts soon realize that something extraordinary has occurred to the Christian because of their kindness, love, sincerity, and integrity.

People around the Christians observe changes in the latter; their demeanor, speech, disposition, and mindset. They begin to produce life all around them because they have received a living gospel in their souls. When a sinner is converted to a saint by the power of the gospel, everyone who belongs to them benefits.

The Christian, therefore, rejoices and shares the gospel through words and deeds just as Jesus Christ's disciples did when they received bread and fish from the hands of their Master and shared them among the crowds:

"And they all ate and were satisfied. And they picked up twelve small hand] baskets full of the broken pieces left over." (Mark 14:20).

Unfortunately, some Christians confirm the ancient proverb: *"The chef's wife and children sleep on an empty stomach."* Such Christians do a world of excellence a thousand miles away but none at home. We can see from the story of Abraham and the unbelieving Jews that no matter how godly a Christian is, they cannot guarantee that their spouses or descendants will be like them. Many Christians travel far and wide to preach the gospel; however, they have ignored their spouses and children to the point that they are the evilest children in the neighborhood as they grow up in every sort of wickedness. Unfortunately, many pastors and Christians parade around and care for other people's families while neglecting their own families.

If any Christian is going to follow the gospel GPS to deliver the gospel to the ends of the earth, they must start in Jerusalem which is their home. Any gospel children's or adult Sunday school teacher who teaches at church but does not teach their children or family at home is ignoring the gospel GPS.

A Christian who could preach and win millions of sinners for Jesus Christ but fails to preach the same gospel to their family of a handful of people misses the direction of the gospel GPS. The prayer of a father who wraps his hand around his children and petitions for their souls has divine power. Words can never express the power of a mother's prayers as her children kneel around her. It is incomparably greater than preaching to tens of thousands of people in a stadium. Jesus forbids any Christian from allowing their employees to work in their enterprises while they are clueless about the gospel. The Christian who follows the gospel GPS from their home and stops by their brothers and sisters, neighbors, and colleagues on their way to the ends of the world quickly and easily arrives there without realizing how long the journey has been.

"Grace does not run in human blood, and rebirth has nothing to do with blood or human birth."

"The impact of a true Christian is first felt at home. They return home to their own family as a converted person, and the family members immediately notice the difference."

The Rough Route

The distinctive sin of the Jews in Jesus' days, the sin that worsened above all their previous sins, was their rejection of Jesus Christ as the Messiah.

He had been very clearly defined in the prophetic scriptures, and those who waited for Him, such as Simeon and Anna, rejoiced to see Him even in His baby form and acknowledged that God had sent forth His redemption. But because Jesus Christ did not appear with elegance and force, He did not meet the expectations of that sinful generation. The disbelieving Jesus shut their eyes against Him because He lacked the outward adornment of a king as well as the honors of royalty. Because Jesus Christ was "a root out of the dry ground," unbelieving Jews:

"...despised and did not regard Him." (Isaiah 53:3)

The Jews' sin did not end there. They were not satisfied with denying Jesus' Messiahship; they were enraged against Him. They pursued Him His entire life looking for His blood. Those Jews were never satisfied until they had totally fulfilled their diabolical hatred by sitting at the foot of the cross and seeing their crucified Messiah's final throes and dying agonies.

It was reasonable that Jesus' disciples would not want to be in the company of such Jews, let alone speak about a Man the latter despised. Although the bible is quiet on the disciples' thoughts, it is plausible that in their minds, they may have preferred to begin in a faraway nation hoping that if they succeeded, their work at home would be easier. They shut the doors the first night they convened because they were terrified of the Jewish leaders:

"Then on that same first day of the week, when it was evening, though the disciples were behind closed doors for fear of the Jews, Jesus came and sttod among them and said, Peace to you!" (John 20:19).

The Jews had no regard for people as evidenced by their subsequent persecution of Saul of Tarsus whose conversion is one of the testimonies of Christianity's divinity. They saw Saul, who became Paul after his conversion, as their fiercest enemy. When a Jew heard the name, Paul, their blood ran cold. More than forty of them swore an oath to kill him, and the rest of the company seemed to be inspired by the same desire wherever he went.

Paul usually drew large crowds of Gentiles who listened to him intently, but the Jews incited riots and mobs, and he was constantly threatened with death by them. They despised him seeing him as an outcast and traitor to his ancestors' faith.

When Paul became a Christian, the Jews could not trust his sincerity, or if they did, they despised him as a maniac whose lunacy was beyond measure remembering how sincere he had been against Jesus Christ and His disciples. To them, it was malicious. However, by adhering to his Master's command, Paul's kind retaliation was to pray for the Jews; he bore the entire nation on his heart as a burden:

"That I have bitter grief and incessant anguish in my heart." (Romans 9:2)

It was and still is difficult to preach to certain individuals in our families, workplaces, neighborhoods, and especially at church: they have been preached to for so long with little change like the Jews in Jerusalem. However, the gospel GPS is programmed to begin in our Jerusalem. Jerusalem was also the home to notorious sinners capable of assassinating Jesus the Savior. Those who ridiculed Him and spat on Him lived in Jerusalem. However, the merciful Jesus, who freely forgives, ordered the gospel to begin "from Jerusalem".

Also, Jesus, the Omniscient God, foresaw that Jerusalem would be destroyed in a matter of days. The Romans were to come and slaughter men, women, and children, tear down the walls, and leave no stone unturned.

Sin has wounded countless sinners, and they are dying; their wounds are bleeding; the heavenly surgeon commands every Christian to bind the wounds first in our Jerusalem. Others who are not as seriously wounded can wait a little longer, but those in our Jerusalem must be served first or perish from their wounds.

It is critical that we operate on sound principles in all of our endeavors; otherwise, our efforts will be futile because success may not be achieved. It is imperative that Christians follow sound principles and follow the right GPS when proclaiming the gospel; otherwise, we will be frustrated. If a traveler to Africa believes that they can reach Accra by traveling swiftly towards Canada, they will most likely fail, even if they use the fastest jet. Let us begin boldly preaching the gospel from our Jerusalem where we can expect resistance. And if we encounter resistance while following the gospel GPS, we should overcome it as Jesus and His disciples did. They loved those who treated them the very worst. In the gospel, the greatest sinners receive the greatest package. If a sinner murders us in our Jerusalem in passion, may we "murder" them with our loving prayers.

"The prayer of a father who wraps his hand around his children and petitions for their souls has divine power."

CHAPTER 11

NAMES

A name is a medium through which someone is identified. Socrates, the philosopher, said: *"Man, know thyself."* So many people think self-knowledge is supposed to be the ultimate type of knowledge, yet it is not. Every good person wishes they could have the good word of all their fellow humans. The foundation of social peace is having families, friends, and neighbors say good things about one another. However, while speaking well of ourselves is good and pleasant in and of itself, sin in our world has destroyed it and turned it into a "woe" when all men speak good of us:

"Woe unto you, when all men shall speak well of you! For so did their fathers to the false prophets." (Luke 6:26).

But still, the desire for a reputable name persists in all of humanity. It is an innate core principle in every human mind, and it so often remains alive when all other charitable practices have ended.

All else being equal, every human being, whether white, black, rich, poor, educated, uneducated, or otherwise, wishes to be known and respected by our fellow humans. We extend our knowledge of our lives beyond our individual minds of being by writing books, inventing ideas, and living a wide range of other impactful lives because we want future generations to remember us, if not long, at least, for a short time after we die. Aside the fear of death, the most terrifying thought that partitions many human souls is the fear that their names will be dehumanized when they die.

The world's Hall of Fame might have "good names" inscribed on its breastplate. There are heroes, writers and poets, noble darers, musicians, and others, from both past and present times, who have had their names engraved in museums, art centers, cemetery tombs, and so on. Many celebrities would not want the earth leveled over their tombs quickly after they are buried. They would not have their final resting place forgotten. They would not have the last visible signs of their life erased from the world's memory. Such a desire to have a good name persists secretly in every human soul, and we only need to look into our own hearts to find it always there in living authority and domineering power.

Know The Name Of Your God

The parallel between God, the Father, who created us in His image and likeness, and the human desire to have their names remembered is striking! God's highest and most important goal is to give Himself a glorious and eternal name. And the main objective of humanity is to glorify and enjoy God. Because He is worthy of being known, God may desire to give Himself a name—that is, to make Himself known. There is no other name that deserves to be known among humanity. There is none like unto Him. There is no one who can stand in His place. God deserves to be known, and making a name for Himself is an admirable ambition for His behavior. God is God; He is compassionate and loving toward His creatures, and there is no better way for Him to bless them than to make Himself known to them.

Unfortunately, because many Christians do not know their God-given names, they also do not know God's name. Satan uses many tricks to divert Christians' attention from the most important and vital matters such as knowing God's name, by suggesting trivial issues to consider. Therefore, *"Human, knowing your God!"* is far a wise precept; for knowledge of God far excels all other knowledge. And God's true and applied knowledge is wisdom which is the mother and midwife of godliness, love, unity, and peace

But how much do we know about God? Nothing but what He has graciously revealed through the Bible, Nature, and, most importantly, His Son, Jesus Christ. Knowing God, the Father, in His Son Jesus Christ, is to love the Father, and being loved by God is the cause of the world being made to know Him (John 3:16). Jesus proclaims the Father's name so that the entire world will recognize and love Him. When we see the Father in the Son, we are filled with both guidance and love.

Knowing God's deity and understanding what it means to say He is God is the most powerful argument for obedience and worship levied on the Christian's soul.

The Name "God"

God created humans, and the creature should naturally become intimately familiar with their Creator just as every child knows their parent's name; we should know Him as God the Father. But because of our soul's blindness, the evilness brought about by the Fall, and each person's sin, there is none who understands, none who seeks after God:

"As it is written, None is righteous, just and truthful and upright and conscientious, no, not one." (Roman 3:10).

Humanity, with their wisdom, created gods of a different kind. Thus, the world had no knowledge of the God known as the "Righteous Father". God is the source of all that is good, true, righteous, superior, and loving. He is not only the Giver of "every good and perfect gift", but He is also the totality and content of all blessings; and human beings know their God is for the ultimate good of all the creatures He has created.

Evidently, in our world, it is incontestable that humanity will never enjoy God's blessings and thus, be in a functional state until we know our God and are at peace with Him.

A person who is willfully completely ignorant of God is in a foggy state of mind, and because they love ignorance, it is obvious that their mind is biased against good. Their willful ignorance of God demonstrates their hatred for Him. When a person opposes God, they cannot be happy, righteous, or safe: they cannot be when they oppose God, who is excellent in holiness and love.

In order to be saved from our sins and ignorance, humanity needed to know God. As a result, when Jesus Christ came to save us, He made it a part of His mission to reveal the Father to the world:

"I have declared unto them thy name and will declare it." (John 17:26 KJV)

Jesus, thus, fulfilled an Old Testament promise:

"I will declare Your name to my brethren; in the midst of the congregation will I praise you" (Psalm 22:22).

He revealed to the world God's glory which shines in His own face:

"In the beginning [before all time] was the Word (Christ), and the Word was with God, and the word was God Himself. And the Word (Christ) became flesh (human, incarnate) and tabernacle (fixed His tent of flesh, lived awhile) among us..." (John 1:1/14).

Jesus understood that the world could not love a God they did not know because love requires knowledge. A sinner who is blind of the soul cannot perceive God and, thus, cannot be touched by His loveliness no matter how lovely He is. So, just as a teacher imparts knowledge to students, Jesus, who is privy to the Father's knowledge, took the time to teach His disciples the Father's name. He worked hard to introduce the Father to them:

"I have made Your Name known to them and revealed Your character and Your very Self, and I will continue to make [You] known, that the love which You have bestowed upon Me may be in them [felt in their hearts] and that I [Myself] may be in them." (John 17:26).

The word "name" refers to the existence of God, the nature of God, the character of God, God's work, and God's revelation. The word "name" is a particularly expressive word in Scripture encompassing all that is properly described about a person. In this case, it includes all of God, and Jesus Christ came to fully reveal God to us.

The highest, the weightiest, and the most righteous reasons for man's yielding up His entire nature to divine service are encapsulated in the word "GOD." Even so, in many of His prayers, Jesus gives God a testing name — *"O righteous Father..."* (John 17:25). Jesus, at other times, had spoken of God as *"Father"* and also as *"Holy Father"*, but He also calls Him — *"O righteous Father."* The knowledge of God as a righteous Father serves as a litmus test for determining whether a Christian truly and spiritually knows God or has only a speculative and lateral concept of Him.

God is "righteous" with the characteristics of a Judge and a Ruler: just, unbiased, who does not spare the guilty. He is also a "Father"—a close relative who is merciful, understanding, loving, tender, and forgiving.

In dealing with His children, God combines His two personalities and acts as both a Judge and a Father in one. While the unbeliever struggles to accept the truth that God is both a Judge and a Father, Christians appreciate the truth that in Jesus Christ's sacrifice on the cross, God's two characters have become one.

When Jesus cried out, *"It Is finished"*, Mercy and justice married, and righteousness kissed his bride's obedience. We see how God is "righteous" and yet a "Father" in the sacred substitution: In the magnificent events of Calvary, God manifested all the love of a tender Father's heart and all the justice of an unbiased judge's gavel. In this context, God simply means "righteous" and yet "Father".

THE HOLY SPIRIT IS NO LESS A PERSON IN THE TRIUNE GOD

The, Father, the Son and the Holy Spirit have such a close relationship with one another so much so that to know the Holy Spirit, we must first know the Son of God and the Father. Thus, a Pentecostalized Christian knows the Holy Spirit by knowing Jesus; by knowing Jesus, they know the Father.

Many Christians are so used to talking about the Holy Spirit's impact and His holy activities and graces that they forget that the Holy Spirit is a Person—that He is a Self-Sufficient Person; or one Person in the nature of the Godhead. Many Christians can think of God, the Father, as a Person because naturally, every human being, whether a Christian or not, may see God as a Teacher who instructs the world through nature. Those acts are such as they can be easily visibly identified and related to. So, humans unconsciously consider the thrilling changes in nature with an eye toward the outer world and the inner and spiritual world as acts of God, the Creator.

Every year, at the end of December, the entire world, regardless of religious beliefs, is unconsciously engaged in congratulating itself and expressing its personalized wishes for Jesus Christ's birth, whether they are careful to say: "Merry Christmas" or "Happy Holidays". And Christians, with a far deeper reverence, seek a new birth of our Savior in our hearts so that as Jesus Christ is already "birthed in us the hope of glory"; we would be "revived in the spirit of our souls".

Thus, in our minds' eye, we return to our spiritual nativity's Bethlehem and carry out the necessary, our first works, and behold Him who is born of lowly parents, laying in a manger, and wrapped in swaddling clothes.

There, Christians, we see our Jesus' glory lurking beneath the swaddling bands; we relive our former loves and celebration with Him as we did in the holy, happy, delightful days of our conversion.

All the events surrounding Jesus' birth: the arrest, the scourging, and the crucifixion are easily imagined by any Christian because we recognize Him, the Son of Man, as a real person, bone of our bone, and flesh of our flesh. However, many Christians have developed the habit of perceiving the Holy Spirit as an outgrowth from the Father and the Son rather than as a Person in His own right. It is partly because the Holy Spirit's operations are so mystical, His actions are so inaccessible, and His acts are so removed from everything that is of sense and of the body. Therefore, Humans cannot easily grasp the concept of His being a Person.

However, the Holy Spirit is a Person. He is not simply a manifestation, an impact, or a flow of something arising from the Father. But He is just as much a Real Person with a name as God, the Father, or God, the Son.

The Name Of Jesus – The Foundation Of Hope And The End Of Hopelessness

A person's name encompasses their personality as well as everything that their name stands for and reflects. A baby has no personality, and their names are meaningless at first. It has not demonstrated any behavior that would distinguish it in anyone's mind. However, as the child grows into adulthood, their name gradually comes to mean more. All of the events of a person's childhood, youth, and early years are then incorporated into their personality.

No parent can accurately predict what their children will become in the future. The very least a parent can do is name their child after someone whose life they want their child to emulate. In contrast to the norm, Jesus came not to be given a name but to fulfill one that had already been assigned to Him. His name represents His Person, Character, and Work; His teaching represents the Christian's faith and hope. He has other titles and relationships. Names indicate things to Him:

"...and His name shall be called Wonderful, Counselor, the Mighty God, the everlasting Father, the Prince of Peace" (Isaiah 9:6c).

Jesus is also called "Emmanuel", "God with us". (Matthew 1:23). Among all the names He is known by, *Jesus* is His own name, and the Father gave Him the name; so, it is the best name that He could bear. The Father, the Son, and the Holy Spirit always have wonderful intercommunion and fellowship. The Father bestowed the Son with His name; the Son revealed the name of the Holy Spirit to the world; and the Holy Spirit glorifies the Son. God, the Father, would not give His beloved Son a name of little or no significance, or a name with a whiff of dishonor. *Jesus* is the highest, brightest, and noblest of names. God gave the best name that any son of man could bear to the best that was ever born of woman. God, through the angel, revealed the name Jesus first to Joseph, a carpenter, a humble man, a working man, unknown and unremarkable except for the justice of his character:

"And her [promised] husband Joseph, being a just and upright man and not willing to expose her publicly and to shame and disgrace her, decided to repudiate and dismiss (divorce) her quietly and secretly. But as he was thinking this over, behold, an angel of the Lord appeared to him in a dream, saying, Joseph, descendant of David, do not be afraid to take Mary [as] your wife, for that which is conceived in her is of (from, out of) the Holy Spirit." (Matthew 1:19-20).

It is, thus, not a name to be dominated by the ears of monarchs, senators, priests, soldiers, white, black, old, young, poor, or wealthy men: It is a name made a household word among the general public. The name of Jesus was sweet at first because of the words that accompanied it; for they were meant to relieve Joseph's confusion, and some of them ran thus—"Fear not".

No name can truly dispel fear like Jesus' name: It is the foundation of hope and the end of hopelessness. Even when He was given the name Jesus, Human eyes had not seen His full human because He was concealed; but He soon came forth having been born of Mary by the power of the Holy Spirit, and an exceptional Man. Although Jesus had human nature, He did not have human corruption. He was born in the image of sinful flesh, but His flesh had no sin.

JESUS THE NAME THAT SAVES

God gave His Son the name *Jesus* for a reason: *"She will bear a Son, and you shall call His name Jesus [the Greek form of the Hebrew Joshua, which means Savior]..." (Matthew 1:21ab)*

The meaning of Jesus' name is "Savior" but it has a deeper meaning concealed within it:

"... for He will save His people from their sins." (Matthew 1:21c).

Jesus or *Joshua* are names that refer to a Savior; so, the full Word is "Jehovah Savior"; and the short version is "Savior". Now, Jesus "saves"—not in the sense of a momentary and common salvation from enemies and troubles as God did through Moses, Joshua, Gideon, David, and others to deliver the Israelites from the hands of their enemies. He saves the world from spiritual enemies, particularly sin. One of the mysteries of the Christian religion is to embrace Jesus as God who became a Man and came to die to save humanity. So, returning to God, the Father, who knows His Son the best, sees *saving* as His Son's defining characteristic, that He is a Savior and is best represented by the name *Jesus*.

God, who cannot make a mistake, refers to His Son Jesus as a Savior. As a result, Jesus, as a Savior, must be on a large scale, continuously, powerfully, and noticeably. At the very announcement of His birth, Jesus' mother sang:

"And my spirit rejoices in God my Savior." (Matthew 1:47).

In its Hebrew form, *Jesus* means *"the salvation of the Lord"* or *"the Lord of salvation"* or *"the Savior"*. The Angel translates it as *"He shall save";* and the Word "He" is emphatic. The word "save" has so many different meanings that expressing its full and exact force is difficult.

Jesus is salvation in the sense of both deliverance and preservation.

He provides health; He is all that is beneficial to humanity; and He saves them in the widest and most comprehensive sense.

Long before Jesus Christ, the Jews were looking for a Savior. They hoped for and anticipated a leader who would free them from the yoke of the Roman Empire and deliver them from servitude to a foreign power. Therefore, after all the teachings Jesus had given to His disciples, they still asked Him before His accession about the supposed political restoration:

"So when they were assembled, they asked Him, Lord, is this the time when You will reestablish the kingdom and restore it to Israel? (Acts 1:6)

The saving that Jesus provides is of a more spiritual nature. He breaks a much more severe yoke by saving humanity from its sins. In His childhood, He was known as Jesus – *"The Holy Child Jesus."* (Acts 4:30).

Jesus went up to the temple with His parents and sat down with the teachers listening to them and asking them questions. In His active life, He was also known as Jesus by His enemies and friends.

Yes, Jesus, as an adult Teacher, is a Savior who, in the very first principles of His doctrine, frees men's minds from superstitious beliefs.

He set them free from the traditions of the fathers scattering the seeds of truth with His lovely hand, the elements of a glorious liberty that will free the human mind from the iron bonds of false philosophy and heretical teachings.

Jesus, the Savior, healed the sick, raised the dead, and saved Peter from drowning. In all of Jesus' middle-life teachings, in those arduous three years of meticulous service, in His public ministry and private prayer, He remained Jesus, the Savior. Just as Joshua used God's power to lead the Israelites into the Promised Land and drive out the Canaanites, Jesus, the Captain of our salvation, will surely bring all Pentecostalized Christians into Heavenly Canaan driving out every enemy.

"Knowing God's deity and understanding
what it means to say He is God
is the most powerful argument
for obedience and worship
levied on the Christian's soul."

Paraclete, The Personal Name Of The Holy Spirit

We have one God: the Father, the Son, and the Holy Spirit, One in Three and Three in One, and the Trinity in Unity always works together.

God sent an angel to name Jesus even before the Holy Spirit, through Mary, conceived Him in the womb:

"Thou shalt call his name JESUS, for He shall save His people from their sins." (Matthew 1:1 KJV).

And when Jesus arrived, He fulfilled the name that had already been assigned to Him. As part of His mission, Jesus named God, the Father, to humanity who should have known God as a Father but did not. After the unspeakable Gift of God ascended to heaven, Jesus was followed by the similarly irreplaceable gift of the Holy Spirit. However, before Jesus' accession and the Holy Spirit's arrival in the world, the former gave His disciples the latter's name:

"But when the Paraclete has come, whom I will send unto you from the Father…" (John 15:26).

The name of the Third Person of the Blessed Trinity, which is familiar to Christians, is "the Spirit" or "the Holy Spirit". His description corresponds to His spiritual, nonmaterial existence and His pure personality as being supremely holy in Himself and His works. The term "Holy Spirit" is His personal title, and His official title is the "Comforter".

The personal name by which Jesus introduced the Holy Spirit to His disciples is The Parakletos, which translates to "Paraclete" in English.

Nowadays, the name Parakletos is used as a verbal adjective to describe someone who is called to assist in a court of law. However, it is extremely difficult to fully explain the meaning of the word Paraclete to anyone. It is a word that embodies so much in such a narrow area. Its convenience is strict, even primitive, and yet it interprets amazing things. In both biblical and literal terms, Paraclete means "called to" or "called beside" another to support them. It is practically synonymous verbally, but not in a sense, with the Latin word advocatus which alludes to someone who is summoned to speak for us by beseeching our lawsuit or legal cases.

Paraclete is a word with far too many meanings to be substituted for any single word in any language. It is broad, and I hope to rephrase the name rather than interpret it. Now, because we have come to use the word "advocate" in a different context, Paraclete, while conveying a portion of the meaning, does not contain it entirely. The word "Paraclete" embodies both "advocate" and "comforter". So, in this context, the meaning of the word "Paraclete" can be divided into two categories: "called to" and "calling to".

The Paraclete is called to assist Christians, help infirmities, recommend, advocate, direct, etc. He is also the One who, as a result, calls to us, for our benefit, a Monitor. Thus, the Paraclete is the Christian's Teacher, Reminder, Motivator, and Comforter. His work as One called to help us is primarily in His strengthening us through rebuke, guidance, inspiration, and other works that would fall under the purview of a comforter or a teacher. In life, I believe we need a "Comforter" and a "Teacher" besides our salvation.

PARACLETE, THE COMFORTER

Before Jesus Christ's first coming, all the spiritual people among the twelve tribes of Israel were waiting for His appearing to console them. Indeed, Jesus was and is the Day-Star, warning the darkness and prophesying the rising sun to Israel before His actual appearance. The Israelites looked to Jesus with the same hope that motivates and encourages the nightly security officer from his lonely post when he sees the brightest stars of the early hours of the day. Thus, Simeon, when he set his eyes on the Baby Jesus, he called Him "…the consolation of Israel." (Luke 2:25).

When Jesus was on earth, He was a source of comfort to all who were blessed enough to be His friends and acquaintances. How often the disciples would run to Jesus Christ to tell Him of their hurts, disappointments, sorrows, and abuses is imaginable. And thoughts cannot conceive how lovingly, with an inimitable tonality of His voice, Jesus would speak to them, encourage them, and cast their fears away.

The disciples regarded Jesus as their Father, and they brought to Him their every need, whine, tantrum, sorrow, and misery. And Jesus, the Great and Wise Physician with an answer and cure for every wound, mixed a concoction for their every treatment: Spiritual, Emotional, Physical, Psychological, and Financial. He, indeed, easily dispensed countless mighty remedies to help alleviate all the fever of all problems.

Jesus, who had been a Human Comfort, had to depart for other great prophecies and great purposes to be fulfilled. So, His physical departure from the world necessitated the arrival of the Paraclete, also known as the Comforter.

THE LOVING PARACLETE

God, the Holy Ghost, is a very loving Comforter. Amma, for over two decades had been in distress and needed consolation. Some passers-by who heard her sorrow, instead of consoling her, judged her. A professional therapist turned up and began to console Amma in her grieving. She did an excellent job by stepping in. However, she had never been through the painful experience Amma had experienced. So, she could not identify with Amma. There, the therapist sat with Amma for hours upon hours attempting to cheer Amma up.

She spoke comforting words to Amma, but she did not love Amma. Amma had never met her. And the therapist was completely disinterested in the former. Notwithstanding her salary, the therapist had only come in to test her abilities. And what was the ramification? The therapist's words ran over Amma like oil over a piece of granite or like the rain pattering on the rock. They did not break Amma's grief; it remained as resolute as ever because the therapist had no love, empathy, or sentiments for Amma.

But then, there was Amma's Father who loved her as much as he loved his own life. As soon as he started talking to Amma, his words became Amma's favorite song which tasted like her favorite food. Amma's Father knew the code to his daughter's heart's doors, and his daughter's ear was tuned in to every word of his. Amma captured the tone of voice of each vowel sound of her Father as it dropped, as it is like the harmonious, loving relationship of a father and daughter.

In love, there is a voice that speaks in its own dialect. Love's voice has a phraseology and an accent that no one else can imitate. Worldly wisdom cannot try to mimic the voice of love, nor can eloquence. Only love has the power to reach the grieving heart. Love is the only towel or tissue that can wipe away a grieving's tears.

Amma's Father's name is the Paraclete, the Loving Comforter whose love for Amma is unimaginable. He absolutely loves Amma and all humans, especially those to whom He was sent.

The Paraclete who loves Amma and all Christians comforts us lovingly and faithfully. Love can be inconsistent at times, but the Paraclete is a constant and unchanging Comforter. He loves well, He has always loved us, and He will always love His own.

During the Paraclete's comforting sessions, His words mask the Christian's sorrows because He knows what to say and when to say it. Because of His genuine love for us, He is the perfect Comforter for all Christians.

Paraclete, The Teacher

While on earth, Jesus Christ was the Authoritative Teacher of His disciples. Except for Jesus Christ, no one was given the title Rabbi. The disciples did not sit at the feet of any other human being to learn their doctrines; rather, they received them directly from the mouth of Him who "spoke as never man spoke". While He stood at Pilate's palace, Pilate asked Jesus:

"Then You are a King?" (John 18:37a).

Jesus effectively responded:

"[You speak correctly!] For I am a King. [Certainly I am a King!] (John 8:37b).

Pilate's ears must have been pricked by Jesus' claim to kingship. Jesus was undoubtedly worn, sorrowful, and frail in appearance. He had spent the first half of the night in agony in the garden. At midnight, He was dragged from Annas to Caiaphas and then from Caiaphas to Herod. The soldiers had not allowed Him to rest until daybreak. From all appearances, Jesus must have appeared to be anything but a king. He sounded and looked like some poor, rough unkempt man on the street who was claiming to be "a king".

But, while Jesus is the King of kings and the Lord of lords, when He said to Pilate: "You say that I am king", He was not referring to His divine Kingship or Rule. Rather, He declared that His kingdom was the primary goal of His life:

"This is why I was born, and for this I have come into the world, to bear witness to the Truth." (John 18:37c).

In effect, Jesus declared that the most important feature of His Kingdom is truth and that He wields royal power over men's hearts through the truth. Truth is absolutely powerful when it is embodied. And Jesus Christ does not merely speak the truth; He taunts the truth. Truth has power over flesh and blood because it is embodied in flesh and blood through the birth of Jesus.

When such a Teacher as Jesus was on leave from His classroom, He could not have had a Pharisee, Sadducee, Gamaliel, or anyone else continue the infallible oracle lectures He had begun. Jesus, the Omniscient and Omnipotent Paraclete or Teacher, could not find anyone like Himself except another Paraclete, even the Holy Spirit. The Paraclete is the absolute Teacher of all Christians. By His own will, the Father begets us through the word of truth (Jesus). He is another Teacher and will be the one to explain Scriptures. The Paraclete will be God's authoritative oracle bringing all darkness in our souls to light. He will untangle mysteries, disentangle all twists of revelation, and make Christians understand what we could not understand without His involvement.

The Paraclete teaches Christians the truth which is Jesus Christ: God's testimony about Jesus Christ and His Son is the truth. And the work of the Paraclete in the heart of humanity is to work in us the truth that leads to salvation.

The knowledge of the truth is comprehensive. As a result, Jesus said: "The Truth" without referring to all truths. Though knowing the truth about anything is a good thing, and we should not be satisfied with a falsity on any point, not every truth will save a human being.

A sinner is not saved by knowing any one theological truth because there are some theological truths that are relatively speaking of lesser value.

Many truths are not vital or necessary, and a man can know them and still not be saved. What Jesus calls "The truth" is what saves the soul from hell.

I pray that every Christian would yearn to know the truth because the perfect truth in human form has the Paraclete's power to impact and transform the sinful world. Truth spoken is conquered, but truth acted out in the life of a Pentecostalized Christian is omnipotent; kudos to the Paraclete's Spirit.

"Worldly wisdom cannot try to mimic the voice of love, nor can eloquence. Only love has the power to reach the grieving heart. Love is the only towel or tissue that can wipe away a grieving's tears."

Epilogue

Jesus Christ kept His personal ministry almost entirely within the borders of Palestine, and He instructed His disciples to begin preaching the gospel in Jerusalem. Because of the narrowness of their nationality, most of the apostles had to take a long time to bring the gospel to anyone other than Jews. Thus, Jews had a full opportunity to know the gospel; however, they were blinded by sin and racist attitudes and, thus, could not see Jesus Christ.

Paul and the other apostles turned to the Gentiles because the Jewish people judged themselves unworthy of eternal life. Thus, Jews' rejection of the gospel made it possible for every Christian to receive the gospel in a way beyond what the power of humans could convey it to us. Although we all heard the gospel preached to us by humans, the Holy Spirit Himself applied the "Word" to our hearts. Even the most zealous Christians cannot preach and impress the gospel on sinners in order to bring it home to their hearts and regenerate, convert, and sanctify them.

Thus, the Holy Spirit leads the sinner into all truth and shines a light on the eternal and the mysterious. In some cases, He takes it very personally. There is a distinct act of God, the Holy Spirit, by which the instrumentality is made effective and the truth is made active in our souls. There is no Christian who received the gospel by heritage. A Christian may be the child of Christian parents, but they are not the children of God.

"What is born of [from], the flesh is flesh [of the physical is physical]; and what is born of the Spirit is spirit." (John 3:6).

If precautions are not taken, someone who claims to be a Christian simply because their parents are Christians may gain a foothold and progress in the church. Contrary to Scripture, such people skip personal confessions of faith (Romans 10:10). That unconfessed faith leads to birthright membership which is fatal to any Christian community wherever it becomes the standard.

Dear Beloved Christian, (speaking to myself and everyone as individuals rather than the nation as a whole) I beseech you to take care that while you can hear the gospel, you can also receive it and proclaim it.

I humbly remind every Christian who is now able to hear the gospel that the "gospel" which is to be told to every human being, is the great truth that:

"It was God [personally present] in Christ, reconciling and restoring the world to favor with Himself, not counting up and holding against [men] their trespasses [bit cancelling them], and committing to us the message of reconciliation (of the restoration to favor)." (2 Corinthians 5:19).

Though all Christians cannot literally preach in the ordinary sense of the word "preach", Jesus' command "Go ye into all the world" is for all Christians. Therefore, we must all bear the gospel to the world in one way or the other. Our preaching may take various forms, but every Christian must preach by living godly lives. Others must preach by talking to the ones and twos, just as Jesus Christ did at Jacob's well where He also interacted with the woman of Samaria. Other Christians may preach on the shores of the lake of Gennesaret as Jesus Christ did, and utter teachings as brilliant in that small village of Sychar as He did at the beautiful gate of the temple. Other Christians should preach by disseminating the truth printed for distribution, which is a truly noble service, especially when the true word of life, the Bible itself, is planted beginning from our Jerusalem to the ends of the world.

If we are unable to speak in our native tongue, we must borrow other Christians' languages; and if we are unable to write in our native tongue, we must borrow other Christian pens; at all costs, we must do so in some way. The essence of Jesus' command is that we must make the gospel known to every soul in some way—throw it in their path, let them know there is a gospel, and persuade them to learn what it means.

No Christian can make a sinner accept or believe the gospel—that is the work of the Holy Spirit—but we can and must make sinners aware of it and plead with them to receive it. However, every Christian must take care that a sinner does not reject the gospel or Christianity because of their ungodly attitude.

May every Christian, through the power of Pentecost, do everything within their power to make every soul aware of the gospel so that even if a sinner does not accept it, they will have had the kingdom of God brought near them. The responsibility of a sinner's accepting or rejecting the gospel is then theirs, not a Christian's. That, then, is Jesus Christ's commission to His disciples *"Go ye into all the world, and preach the gospel to every creature"* fulfilled.

Acknowledgment

I am exceedingly grateful to God for making me see much benevolence in action toward me. I gratefully ascribe all glory not to my own effort but to God's grace, mercy, and goodness.

Anyone who knows me well would attest that my life is chock-full of examples of the truth David stated in the following words:

"Your gentleness and condescension have made me…" (Psalm 18:35b).

God's condescension can serve as a comprehensive interpretation of my whole life. It is God's making Himself little, which is the cause of my being able to do anything. I am so little that if God should have manifested His greatness without condescension, I should be trampled under His feet. But God, who must stoop to view the skies and bow to see what angels do, has been gracious to me to bend His eye yet lower and look to the lowly and the contrite and give me grace.

The God who does not sell grace or glory, He who does not put them up to auction to those who can give something in return for them in His robes of grace has been merciful to meet me on the ground of being a nobody and undeserving, and said to me: "I will be gracious unto you." He has given me grace without money, grace without price, and grace without any merit in me. My prayer is to continually love you, God, more than anyone and anything in the world.

Dad, who is now in heaven, you know that I would if I could give everything to maintain an unbroken and intimate fellowship with you. But alas, in this world, our bodies are subject to death, so we do not get or become what we always wish for. While on earth, you were a testimony to what God can do for her daughter through a father. Thank you, Dad, for looking beyond yourself to care for other people's welfare. Love you, Dad! But you do not have the right to be asleep for this long, for your beloved daughter misses you.

To my family: Dads, Moms, Aunts, and Siblings, you know I have a deep love for you for who you all are to me. And I express my appreciation to you all.

For their untold hours of editing and sharing of ideas, I express my heartfelt thanks to Rev. Vincent Davies. You have been a great blessing to me. Without your commitment, this book could not have been completed. To Apostle Dr Ben Debrah (National Head Sweden Australia, Church of Pentecost), Apostle Dr. Frank Asirifi(National Head Guyana, Church Of Pentecost), Elder Philip Asare (New York District Secretary, Church of Pentecost), Deaconess Lilian Martey (New York Evangelism, Church of Pentecost), Mrs. Henrietta Anim-Ansah - nee Amoako-Asante (Church of Pentecost, New York District). Derek Owusu (Church Of Pentecost Bethel District Youth), Mary Elizabeth Gyamfi (Church of Pentecost, New York District Sunday School Deaconess Christy Mensah, Deaconess Agnes Bediako, Deaconess Juliana Ohene, Deaconess Doreen Osei Boah, Deaconess Roselle Duah, Deaconess Esther Fremah, Deaconess Patricia Appiah, Deaconess Doris Akoamoah, Aunty Sarah Adarkwah I convey my heartfelt gratitude, which words are not able to express, to you.

You grabbed the vision and would not let go; despite incredible deadline pressures, you read the necessary material to be able to write an endorsement for the book. Thank you for making God's vision your vision. Whenever I think about what you have done, I envision that day when we all, in a loving fellowship as a church, will come to the great gathering of God, the holy convocation of saints of every tongue, the central home of all the tribes of His great family.

Your collective contribution has well been for solemn purposes; for it is an act for joyous purposes; a solemn joy, a holy delight for the restoration of broken marriages, families, homes, and the world. I humbly pray that God will forever remember what you have done and bless you accordingly. You have brought me joy.

I am indebted to every priest and wife of the Church of Pentecost and beyond for your godly example. I humbly thank all ministers and wives of the Church of Pentecost, USA INC. I appreciate their indirect role in gracing every word in the book and providing advice. I can never stop thinking of the generous advice, consolations, and encouragement that some women and men in my life rendered to me when I needed it most. You have prayed with me to advance this worthy cause. There is wisdom in many counselors. Your love, prayers, and advice are invaluable.

I am grateful to all of you who have shared your personal experiences regarding Singleness, Marriage, Family, etc. Your testimonies will not only inspire others, but they will also make this book more appealing. They provide not only informative examples but also spectacular key points along the journey. It's mesmerizing! Thank you very much.

As I put down my pen for the last time, I humbly offer a blessing to everyone who reads this book. May the grace of our Lord Jesus Christ and the Son of God be with you. May the grace of that exceptional Person who is God and Man in one Person and who is the church's bridegroom continue to be solemnly bestowed on you. May the grace that comes with His supremacy, His kingship, and His divinely human sovereignty come to you all.

My Paraclete (Holy Spirit), I will be forever grateful to You!!!

WELCOME TO OUR PARACLETE FAMILY!!

Whether you received this book as a gift, borrowed it, or purchased it yourself, we are glad you read it. It is just one of the many helpful, insightful, and encouraging resources produced by our Paraclete family.

It began in 2023 with the vision of a Woman, Ewuramma, an author of several books on Marriage, Parenting, Family, Abuse, Friendship. Alarmed by the societal and Religious Unnamed Abuses and the conscious and unconscious hatred and neglect of the needy, Ewuramma has founded Our Paraclete foundation to give voice to the Religious and non-Religious survivors of all kinds of abuse.

Many Christians have long been Christians, have grown rich in experience, and known God's love and faithfulness.

Please, let us look out for the little ones, and speak to them goodly and in comfortable words, whereby they may be cheered and strengthened. When we determine the little ones have weakness, in the plentitude of our wisdom and experience, we need to advice and train them. Let's not withhold graces from them when we have no intention to help them get better and become useful to the family of God and the communities of the world.

Please, let's act in a noble and a virtuous part to cheer the little ones up and bade them of good courage. Some have been wounded not because of their faults but by the people they trusted. Therefore, let's please salute them with words of tender encouragement; for this is precisely what Christians do.

Above all else, let's cease not to pray for the little ones till their little heart is completely and forever given to God. Be a Prophet Samuel to the little ones as he was to David. Be a Naomi to the little ones, and she was to Ruth. Be Elizabeth to the little ones as she was to Mary, for you may be nurturing a king of Israel or a descendant of Jesus Christ, the Savior of the world.

In fact, that is what the Paraclete is all about - providing inspiration, comfort, advocacy, guidance, information, and godly advice to people in all stages of life.

May our Paraclete, the Third Person of the Blessed Trinity, enlighten us so that we will know that we are one family fighting a common enemy called Satan. May He bless us so that we can be a blessing to everyone that comes our way. Amen

EMAIL US YOUR STORY!!!

Please, give us the privilege of hearing how the conversations in SPREADING THE GOSPEL AND THE SPIRIT OF PENTECOST: TO POSSESS THE NATIONS OF THE WORLD have impacted you, your Single Life, your Marriage, your Family or your Loved One.

Email Ewuramma via:
ourparacletefoundation.inc@gmail.com

Our Paraclete Foundation Inc. is a non-profit organization established to bring to remembrance that everyone is the DARLING of God.

Our objective is to let every person know and feel that God loves us unconditionally so that as a natural result, we will love Him in return; and in proportion, as our love knowledge increases, our faith strengthens, and our conviction to love one another deepens, the world will know that we are really ONE FAMILY AND FROM ONE RACE.

I pray that God will grant us the grace so that the very constitution of our being will be constrained to yield our hearts to God into building godly human and marriage relationships.

Appendix

1. The Secret Place – Highway of Love. https://highwayoflove.com/2009/01/16/the-secret-place/

2. Live In The Miraculous - November 23rd-2022| Rhapsody Of Realities TeeVo, 2022. https://www.doxauniversal.org/post/live-in-the-miraculous-november-23rd-2022

3. What We Believe – Harvest Church. https://www.soldoutforjesus.com/what-we-believe/

4. Acts 1:14 - Online Bible - Bible Sprout. https://www.biblesprout.com/bible/acts-1-14/

5. The Source Of The Jordan River | City on a Hill Teaching Center. https://cityonahilltc.org/the-source-of-the-jordan-river-3/

**END OF
VOLUME ONE**

www.ingramcontent.com/pod-product-compliance
Lightning Source LLC
Chambersburg PA
CBHW071920290426
44110CB00013B/1429